GYPSIES

AND

GENTLEMEN

GYPSIES
AND
GENTLEMEN

THE LIFE AND TIMES
OF THE LEISURE CARAVAN

NERISSA WILSON

Columbus Books

London

For Fiver

First published in Great Britain in 1986 by
Columbus Books Limited
19-23 Ludgate Hill, London EC4M 7PD

Designed by Val Hill

British Library Cataloguing in Publication Data
Wilson, Nerissa
    Gypsies and gentlemen: the life and times of the leisure caravan.
    1. Trailer camps—Social aspects
    2. Trailer camps—History   3.Automobiles—Trailers—Social aspects
    4.Automobiles—Trailers—History
    I. Title
    307'.334   GV198.7
    ISBN 0–86287-297-9

Typeset by Falcon Graphic Art Ltd
Wallington, Surrey
Printed and bound by
R.J. Acford, Chichester, Sussex

CONTENTS

1	In the Beginning . . .	7
2	Early Working Caravans	16
3	Gypsies and Tinkers	29
4	Leisure and Pleasure	40
5	Men with a Mission	57
6	Travelling Artists	77
7	The Good Life	83
8	Four-legged Friends	95
9	The Caravan Club	116
10	Caravans for Living	131
11	War and After	139
12	Twentieth-century Travellers	156
13	The Golden Years	168
14	Modern Times	185
	Footnotes	197
	Bibliography	198
	Picture acknowledgements	200

CHAPTER 1

IN THE BEGINNING...

The history of the caravan is not, as you might think, a long saga of gypsy gatherings, desert treks or ancient persecutions. There isn't even a word for caravan in the Romany language. The gypsies and other nomadic tribes travelled, through the centuries, in carts of various degrees of sophistication. Anyone else who moved around usually went by horseback, and spent as little time as possible on the journey. All over the world, and particularly in Britain, the roads were so bad until the nineteenth century that no one travelled on them unless they had no alternative. If travellers attempted to go long distances they were often detained for days on the way because weather conditions made the roads impassable. The stage coaches lumbered up and down the country over surfaces that had not been improved since they were built by the Romans.

Although the first toll gates on the roads were introduced in 1663, little attempt was made to use the money collected to alter the quagmires that connected one town with the next. In 1734, an advertisement for the Newcastle flying coach proudly announced: 'A coach will set out towards the end of next week for London or any place on the road. To be performed in nine days, being three days sooner than any other coach that travels the road, for which purpose eight stout horses are stationed at proper distances.' The roads in Sussex were particularly notorious, and there is a story told about a lady who required six stout oxen to drag her coach to church. People everywhere used to refer to the really muddy pot-hole-ridden patches as the 'Sussex part of the road'.

Even when a passenger was safely ensconced in a coach, and lucky enough to get from one inn to the next without sticking in the mire or capsizing, there was always a danger of highwaymen. They roamed the whole of Britain, and even held up carriages travelling in the middle of London in broad daylight. The roads there were little better than in the provinces. It used to take two hours to drag Queen Caroline's coach from St James' Palace to Kensington.

While the wealthy travelled in discomfort in carriages and stage coaches, the poor stayed at home, or went reluctantly in vehicles that were known from the sixteenth century onwards as caravans. These bore no resemblance to the caravans of today, but were bare, and horribly uncomfortable, with no springs or padding to save the bones from rattling at every jolt. Later, when the railways were introduced, many of these caravans were taken off the road and given iron wheels, so that they could be attached to the trains as third-class carriages. Eventually, these caravans were relegated to the back end of the train, and came to be known, as they are today, as guard's vans.

Commercial travellers rode horses with panniers on either side of their saddles full of their samples, and they moved around in groups to lessen the danger of attacks from robbers. Food was carried in the same way, and often great amounts of perishable goods rotted when harvests were over-abundant. Tinkers and gypsies and circus and menagerie-owners, who were the only people who actually lived on the road, travelled in wagons and pitched tents at night in places well known to them as safe for centuries past. These sleeping grounds had romantic names such as Little Egypt, Gallows Grove and Dead Sophie's Lane. In *The Uncommercial Traveller* Charles Dickens described one of these wayside halts. 'All the tramps – the gypsy tramps, the cheapjack, the show-tramp – find it impossible to resist the temptations of the place, and all turn the horse loose when they come to it, and boil the pot. Bless the place, I love the ashes of the vagabond fires that have scorched the grass.'

The pot would probably have contained boiled meat and potatoes, whether it was breakfast or supper time, and quite possibly the meat would be rabbit, caught by one of the family's lurchers. A good dog was priceless, because it could catch you a rabbit and bring it home and you would not have committed trespass in order to get your meal. The travellers would be very likely on their way to one of the fairs held regularly at different towns and villages every year. Each fair had its own identity and traditions. Since the local population moved around very little, the fair was considered the high point of the year, and people flocked to see the side shows and to buy their goods for the next twelve months. Appleby in Cumbria was the site of the biggest horse fair, and was attended by dealers from a very wide area, but there were many other fairs that also specialized in horse dealing. Mop fairs were held in the autumn at Stratford-upon-Avon and many other towns, and would have been packed with employers searching out men and women who hoped for work, and who mingled in the crowd wearing a symbol of their occupation in their clothing. For example, a thatcher wore a fragment of woven straw, carters and wagoners twisted a piece of whip-cord in their hats, and shepherds carried their sheep-crooks in their hands. The fairs were named after the mops that the women wanting to go into service carried. Once the serious business of the day had been accomplished, the side shows made the occasion into a time of gaiety. Wrestlers and boxers, jugglers and acrobats, freakish dwarves, giants and bearded ladies competed for attention

Men wore a symbol of their trade in their button-holes at the hiring or 'mop' fairs: a twist of wool for shepherds, shipcord for carters, and straw for grooms.

with booths where young men could show off to their girlfriends in games of skill and strength. Menageries were enormously successful. Their owners made vast fortunes if they were willing and able to take the risks involved in paying large sums of money to obtain wild animals.

The first giraffe brought to Britain cost George Wombwell £1,000 and it died within three weeks. George Wombwell was probably the most famous menagerie-owner of them all. There had been menageries since about 1700, small affairs moving around with difficulty over the same pot-holes that bedevilled other travellers, but by 1800 there were many thriving businesses, all in cut-throat competition with each other, touring the fairs and competing for the pennies of the country people. George Wombwell, who was born in 1777, started out by buying two boa-constrictors for £75 and recovered their price in profits in a matter of weeks. He started touring Britain, taking an elephant wagon with him which required thirty horses to drag it up steep hills. One year, at Bartholomew's Fair, his elephant suddenly died. A rival menagerie-owner heard about the death, and quickly drew up a notice which

A successful menagerie-owner could make a fortune by displaying his exotic animals to country people who had never travelled more than few miles from their birthplace. Menagerie-owners were among the first users of caravans.

proclaimed, 'The only living elephant in the fair.' George Wombwell responded with a sign of his own which read: 'Come and see the only dead elephant in the fair.' The public were fascinated, and many more pushed in to see the dead than the living creature.

The crowds at these fairs would probably travel only a few miles during their lifetimes. They walked wherever they went, and saw only what came to them. They mixed very little and kept their local dialects and habits. They were fearful of gypsies and strangers, and would never have dreamed of going anywhere for pleasure or curiosity outside their own small sphere of interest. Apart from fair days, the roads around the villages were used only by the local gentry and professional men. They usually rode on horseback. The judge went round his circuit, and often held up the sessions because of the weather. Clergymen visited their parishioners when duty forced them out. The unpleasant journeys prompted one Devonshire vicar, John Marriott of Broadclist, to write a poem, which began:

In a Devonshire lane, as I trotted along
T'other day much in want of a subject for song,
Thinks I to myself, half inspired by the rain,
Sure marriage is much like a Devonshire lane.
In the first place 'tis long and when once you are in it
It holds you as fast as a cage does a linnet,
For howe'er rough and dirty the road may be found
Drive forward you must, there is no turning round.[1]

As he rode along muttering his poem under his breath, the Reverend Marriott would probably have met very few other people in the lane, and would have known personally everyone in the carts and carriages that he did see. He would have found it worth mentioning when he came home any stranger that he passed. The country was static, although the industrial revolution was already well established. The mills were flourishing, the mines were busy, but the feudal system that had gripped the British for centuries still provided the normal pattern of life for most people. They had a lord of the manor. They worked for him, either directly on the estate and in the big house, or indirectly in the nearby towns and villages. Wealth was judged by possession of land, and with the ownership of estates and farms went all the privileges of power. Men still did not vote unless they were property-owners. Small children worked and school was not compulsory or free, nor even considered desirable by many for the working classes. Life stood still, and no one imagined that anything much would change the established order of things.

Then various events rocked the calm. The first railway train appeared in 1826, closely followed by railway lines connecting various major towns. Suddenly it was possible to move from one place to another. The trains were

Gypsies cooked in the open, using hooks made of hazelwood for holding the cooking-pot over the flames.

originally expected to handle mostly freight, and the carriages for the poor were uncomfortable in the extreme: they were in some cases the old caravans adapted for railway tracks that have already been mentioned. Sometimes the carriages, full of passengers, were left in shunting yards for hours on end, but the possibility of travelling far from home was there at last, and people took advantage of it in increasing numbers.

The steam plough and the threshing machine were introduced, and did the work of an army of farm labourers. In 1856 John Fowler ploughed an acre in one hour using a steam engine. A ploughman would have worked from 6 a.m. to 2 p.m. with a half-hour break for food, and walked ten miles, in order to plough the same acre. Meanwhile John Loudon MacAdam, a Scottish engineer, had become the first person to take up road-making as a career. He developed a system using small pieces of granite as the road surface. Before, lumps of stone were dumped on roads from local quarries and the passing traffic was relied upon to grind the stones gradually down in size. MacAdam began to work in 1815 and was then put in charge of the roads of Scotland and Bristol. He spent thousands of pounds of his own money in his enthusiasm for improvement, and by the mid-nineteenth century steam-rollers appeared in various parts of the country, making the jobs for the road crews easier.

People started to venture out. They went as far as the towns where they found work, and stayed, living in slums which grew at an alarming rate. Factories pumped smoke into the atmosphere relentlessly and women and children grew deformed and died of disease and malnutrition as they slaved over their repetitive tasks. 'Bread was dear and flesh and blood were cheap,' Thomas Hood wrote in his poem 'The Song of the Shirt' in 1842. The value of land fell drastically, power and influence deserted the country and settled in the big industrial towns, with merchants and businessmen. People who were desperate or dissatisfied enough travelled long distances to find new work and new experiences.

For the men and women who had always made their living on the road, conditions improved greatly. They started to carry their belongings about with them and to accumulate more possessions. The kitchen furnaces that Count Romford had recently invented to be used in cottages by the poor were portable enough to be carried inside their wagons so that they could cook and stay warm indoors if they wished. They gradually gave up their tents, putting beds across the ends of their wagons instead and sleeping inside.

The changes to the old wagons happened sporadically, and over a period of years. No one knows who actually invented the first real caravan, but certainly one of the innovators was a Venetian called Antoine Franconi (1738–1836), who was many things during his life, including a bullfighter, a soldier of fortune and the doyen of a travelling circus. He had a show that moved throughout Europe and the Near East. In his old age he designed and

Before the advent of caravans, gypsies lived in tents of bent sapling wood and covered in blankets or felt.

After the business was completed at the hiring fairs, people enjoyed the stalls and festive atmosphere provided by travelling shows and circuses.

lived in a large caravan known as a voiture nomad, which had two separate rooms and a rear balcony. He had the advantage of good Napoleonic French roads to ride along, and he probably lived in his van for several years before men like MacAdam and Thomas Telford had improved the British roads to a standard that made caravanning a practical proposition.

The first mention of an English caravan is in Charles Dickens' *The Old Curiosity Shop*, published in 1840, which introduces one Mrs Jarley, a waxworks proprietress, who rode about in a house on wheels with a stove, a bed and a chest of drawers, all wonderfully orderly and clean. From then on, an extraordinary variety of people, of every class and inclination, took to the roads in their vans.

CHAPTER 2

EARLY WORKING CARAVANS

In an agricultural economy it was not surprising that some of the first caravans were developed for the use of farm workers. For hundreds of years, shepherds had used huts for shelter during lambing time, when they needed to be out all night with their ewes. Some of these huts had been placed on two small wheels, so that they were easier to drag along to the fields. By the middle of the nineteenth century, these were being replaced by four-wheeled caravans which the farm horse pulled to the lambing fold. There is a description of one of these vans in *Far from the Madding Crowd* by Thomas Hardy in which he presents a picture of a rather comical structure, like a little Noah's Ark perched against the skyline, containing a stove, shelves for both animal medicines and bacon, bread and cheese, and a couch of old corn sacks. This interior is lit by a lantern with a candle inside, and by the 'scarlet handful of fire' which reflects 'its own genial colour upon whatever it could reach,' and flings 'associations of enjoyment even over utensils and tools'. This atmosphere of warmth and cosiness, with the flickering light giving beauty to the bottles of turpentine and castor oil, is perhaps a rather optimistic picture of life in one of these huts. It must have been bitterly cold at times, and very lonely.

Although Farmer Gabriel Oak in *Far from the Madding Crowd* sleeps on corn sacks, a more common arrangement would have been a cot with a pen underneath, so that weak lambs could be brought inside to the warmth to build up their strength before returning to their mothers in the fields; so the farmer would have shared his accommodation with them and perhaps his sheep dog, but would have seen no other living creatures for days on end.

These caravans were used all over the world, and not always just for the lambing season. In the United States, where a shepherd was likely to have charge of thousands of sheep spread over vast acres of land, he might well live all the year round with his flock. The vans there were adapted from the early covered wagons of the homesteaders, but eventually developed a standard form which included a stove, bed, benches and cupboards and a folding table. With heat insulation, radios and rubber tyres added, the same caravans can be seen today in use in the United States. In Siberia, shepherds traditionally took their sheep away for six weeks in the summer, going off on five-day shifts to work in pairs, living in the vans and giving the sheep a change of pasture.

Occasionally, English shepherds stayed with their sheep all year round, coming home in the evenings for a meal and to collect the supplies for the next twenty-four hours, but very few farms would warrant such behaviour, since the acreage of most of them was only a fraction of the vast tracts of land in Russia or the United States. It was only during the miserable cold nights of lambing, when the shepherd needed to go round the fold every half hour or so, that he would find it necessary to have his caravan. The hut on wheels purchased by Gabriel Oak costs him £10. Some farmers might have bashed their own huts together from old carts and bits of wood left about the place, but these would have been extremely draughty. The properly-made vans were more comfortable, but the great danger with them was lack of ventilation. They were always equipped with ventilating holes or windows with sliding shutters in the walls or doorway, and in later years the roof was sometimes raised so that windows in the ceiling could allow more light and air. However,

The accommodation in living vans for travelling workmen was sparse, and so home comforts were few and far between.

when the weather turned very nasty and the wind howled in through the holes in the walls, even a prudent farmer like Gabriel Oak might have been foolhardy enough to close the sliding shutters on both sides of his van and to put a sack under the bottom of the door in order to warm up for just a few minutes. With the fire lit, the oxygen would be very quickly used up. Then the occupant's head would begin to ache and throb. Hardy describes such an incident in *Far from the Madding Crowd*. Just before losing consciousness, 'fancying himself weary by reason of the broken rests of the preceding night', Oak decides to 'get up, open the slide, and then allow himself to fall asleep.' He falls asleep, however, 'without having performed the necessary preliminary.' Oak is lucky on this occasion: the beautiful Bathsheba Everdene, passing by his van, hears the dog whining at the door and goes to investigate. Gabriel Oak wakes to find her cradling his head in her lap, has his life saved and loses his heart in the same moment. Other shepherds might well have been less fortunate, and the question of ventilation was one that seriously concerned caravan-users.

Various manufacturers began to build not only shepherds' caravans but

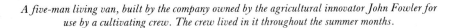

A five-man living van, built by the company owned by the agricultural innovator John Fowler for use by a cultivating crew. The crew lived in it throughout the summer months.

also living vans for men who worked with the new farm machinery for steam ploughing and for men who made up the crew for road rollers and traction engines. At one time three manufacturers, Fowler's, Aveling's and Faulk's, held a competition to test the quality of ventilation in their vans. All the doors and windows were closed, the fire in the stove was lit and a kettle for tea was put on to boil. The winner was to be the man whose kettle boiled first, but the main purpose of the exercise was to make sure that there was enough ventilation in the closed vans to supply oxygen, even with a fire burning and using it up fast, for as long as it took to boil a kettle. Fowler, who was the man who invented the steam plough and had spent all his working life in the industry of farm equipment, was able to claim victory, but this was probably because he had a kettle with a thicker bottom than his opponents. All three manufacturers were highly commended for the design of their vans, all of which stayed ventilated sufficiently long for the kettles to boil, even though the windows were completely steamed up by the end of the competition.

The engineering advances of the mid-nineteenth century excited great public excitement, and the people who pioneered new projects were famous figures. Isambard Kingdom Brunel, who was born in 1806, was a perfect example of the gifted Englishmen of the period who used the products now available because of the Industrial Revolution and helped to speed up the process of industrialization by their work. After building the Bristol suspension bridge, Brunel surveyed the land for the Great Western Railway which would connect Bristol and London. While he travelled up and down the countryside he made use of a travelling carriage called a britschka, a vehicle which stopped just short of being a caravan but had many of its attributes. His britschka was specially adapted to carry plans and engineering instruments and could be fitted up with a bed if necessary. It was a form of carriage that had been in use since the late eighteenth century for professional men like diplomats or road and railway engineers. It, like another carriage known as the dormeuse that was adopted by young men while they travelled on the Continent for the Grand Tour, offered a certain degree of comfort and gave the occupant a chance to keep his things around him, but it was very much a stop-gap solution as a place to sleep.

Brunel would always have chosen to sleep in a hotel if he could, although he wrote complaining letters about the miserable standard of hotel accommodation that he had to suffer while he was working on the railway project. He became a very highly respected figure, as one incident illustrates. When he accidentally swallowed a gold half-sovereign while doing a conjuring trick for some children, the coin lodged in his windpipe and he became gravely ill. A lengthy series of attempts to dislodge the coin by traction and by surgery took place, while the whole country waited with bated breath. When at last the half-sovereign dropped out of his mouth without any further harm being caused, a friend of Brunel's ran through the Atheneum Club in London shouting, 'It's out! It's out!' and everyone knew exactly what he was talking about.

In 1855, during the first winter of the Crimean War, the War Department asked Brunel to design a set of prefabricated buildings to send out to Renkoi in the Crimea as a hospital for the wounded. By the time that Brunel sat down to prepare the drawings for these buildings he would have read the reports that had already filtered back about the appalling conditions and inefficiencies of the campaign. The true horrors of the first winter were vividly described by Russell in *The Times*, in a series of articles that established him as the first war correspondent in the modern sense. Amongst the men stirred to action by those reports was a photographer called Roger Fenton, who travelled out to the Crimea in February 1855 and went round the battlefields in a caravan, recording what he saw on camera.

Roger Fenton had first become interested in photography whilst studying art in Paris. When he realized that he would never be a good enough painter to make a career for himself, he came back to England to be a solicitor; in his spare time he developed his interest in photography, and became a keen amateur. At the time various photographic processes, all very new, were being tried out. The Great Exhibition of 1851 featured an exhibition of photographs from Europe and America which proved very popular; over the next couple of years the various British factions who favoured one type of processing over another, or who jealously guarded patents which prevented others from experimenting with different methods, finally sorted out their differences and in 1853 the Photographic Club and Journal were launched, with the enthusiastic support of Queen Victoria and Prince Albert, who became patrons of the new Photographic Club. They befriended Roger Fenton, and he took a good many pictures of the royal family. The royal couple were so keen on photography that they had a darkroom installed at Windsor, and when Fenton went out to the Crimea he travelled under their patronage, with a letter of introduction from the Prince Consort.

He had used a caravan before, as a travelling darkroom when he took photographs in Yorkshire, and he had his van shipped out with him to Balaclava. The van had originally been a wine merchant's vehicle in Canterbury. It was converted for Fenton into a caravan, with living, cooking and sleeping and darkroom accommodation. Panes of yellow glass with shutters were fitted into the sides, and the bed folded up into a small space under the bench during the daytime hours. Cisterns for distilled and ordinary water were fitted to the top of the van. There was a bookshelf, and special places on the wall for fixing the gutta-percha baths and glass dippers, and for knives, forks and spoons. The kettle and cups hung from the roof, and under the floor was a specially designed trough to receive waste water. Since the van

LIVING VANS.

For use with Road Rollers and Traction Engines.

LIVING VAN, WITH ACCOMMODATION FOR 3 MEN.

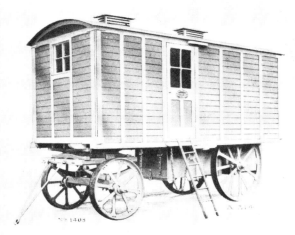

LIVING VAN FOR THE ACCOMMODATION OF 5 OR 6 MEN.

The body is constructed of thoroughly seasoned timber, and mounted on wheels of our Standard design.

The interior of the Van is provided with sleeping berths, beds, bedding, cooking stove, cooking utensils, folding desk, vice and bench, etc. Mosquito-proof doors and windows can be fitted if desired. A chest or cupboard is fitted under the hind part of the Van for stores, etc. We also construct a smaller type of Van for the accommodation of three men (see upper illustration).

Most British caravan firms included information about mosquito-proof doors and windows in their advertisements because their products were bought by companies throughout the Empire.

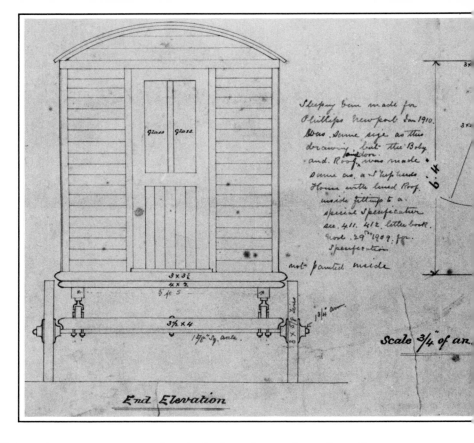

was painted in light colours so as not to absorb the heat it stood out for miles, and often came under fire. No one knew what a caravan was, and people constantly peered at it and clustered round. Fenton ordered the words 'photographic van' to be put on the side to satisfy their curiosity, but was then besieged by soldiers wanting him to take their photograph to send home.

By the time that Fenton took his photographs, conditions in the Crimea had improved considerably, because the hard winter had turned to an early spring and a supply railway had been built. Florence Nightingale had just arrived and was making good use of the new supplies as they came in. Even so, Fenton took some extraordinary pictures of life at war. He was not the first war photographer. That distinction went to an amateur painter living in Bucharest, called Karl Baptist von Szathmari, who had followed the war in a photographic carriage in 1854 and shown his pictures in Paris the next year. However, Fenton's photographs had an enormous impact. The Crimean War was quite extraordinary for many reasons. It was a futile battle. It was the last war in which commissions were purchased and dandy officers abounded. It was the last war in which mortar balls were used, and it was to be forever associated with the bungling of the Charge of the Light Brigade. But it was also the first war to be covered by photographers and newspaper reporters, and to make use of supply railways, telegraphic communications and modern nursing techniques. It combined the same mixture of old and new worlds that

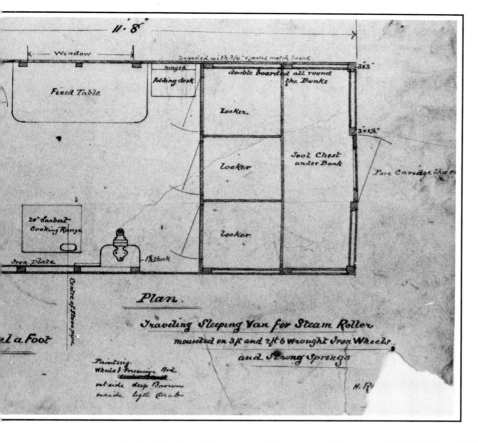

In the late nineteenth century, a sleeping van would cost about £75. Individual specifications were catered for, although standard models were also for sale.

could be found in Britain at the time, and it provided a great opportunity for talented men and women to try out their ideas.

Fenton only managed to remain in the Crimea until June of 1855. He found it physically impossible to work in his caravan once the summer arrived, because the intense heat made the inside of the stuffy darkhouse an oven. The chemicals gave off dreadful fumes and it was impossible to control the temperature sufficiently well to make the printing process successful. Feeling unwell, he went back to England. He would probably not have stayed that long if he had been forced to live in his van all the time he was abroad, so spartan and cramped was its accommodation. In fact, he was entertained royally everywhere he went. He dined sumptuously with generals and officers, sharing with them the luxury of their quarters, which offered a stark contrast to the surroundings of the ordinary soldiers.

Before setting sail, Roger Fenton sold his van for £35. It saved him the problem of shipping it home, and he may have come to hate it after the sessions in the gruelling heat, trying to coax good prints out of over-warm chemicals. He had another made for him in England and for another few years continued to travel round the countryside with it taking photo-

The men who lived in the vans helped to build better roads for other caravans to travel upon.

graphs. Then, in 1862, he suddenly gave up photography altogether.

Meanwhile, continued refinements to the steam-engine made the road rollers, traction engines, steam ploughs and threshers steadily more attractive to the British workforce, and also to their compatriots abroad in the Empire, who read catalogues and magazines and ordered many of the new machines almost as soon as they were invented. Most van-makers mentioned the optional extras for tropical climates, such as mosquito-proof doors and windows, in the literature of their catalogues. The market was almost limitless. There is an early record of a steamroller, built in Birmingham and sent to Calcutta in 1864. This was patented by a man called Mr Batho, in conjunction with a colleague, a Mr W. Clark, a municipal engineer in Calcutta. To ship such an unwieldy object for thousands of miles would have been costly and hazardous, and Mr Clark must have been tremendously excited when he unwrapped this symbol of the new and conquering Empire to which he was proud to belong.

Not many people in Britain could afford to buy their own machines, so the machine-hire business developed and by the 1870s steam-engines were seen all over the countryside. These did not operate on farms in the winter months because they were too heavy for the wet fields, but in March and April the teams set off. Ward and Dale Ltd, of Sleaford, Lincs., formed by two gentlemen farmers in the 1870s, had a fleet of 24 John Fowler steam-ploughs. They sent these out with cultivating crews consisting of five men – a fireman, two engine-drivers, a ploughman and a cook boy. They took a four-wheeled living van with them which served as a cookhouse and five-bunk sleeping place. The interior was plain and serviceable, but perfectly adequate for the housing of their needs. Each team took a pair of engines, a five-furrow plough, an eleven- or thirteen-tine cultivator and a two-wheeled, 250-gallon water cart with them. They worked from dawn to dark, ploughing up to fifteen acres, or cultivating forty acres of land, on a good day. Since they were paid bonuses on the number of acres completed they laboured hard to earn as much money as possible during the summer months.

The caravan was a mixed blessing for the crews of traction engines. It meant that they were on the job and could start early, but they had all the housekeeping to do and needed to take time in the evening to clean and cook. They also had to put up with each other's company in cramped conditions for long periods of time. Some men adapted to the life better than others. There is a story of one Amos Arnold who drove for James Penfold Ltd of Arundel, Sussex, who always made sure that he asked for permission to leave the van in a farmyard, near to where the hens roamed about scratching for food. Before leaving for work in the morning he would scatter a few grains of corn on the floor of the caravan then leave the door ajar, and the crew would return in the evening to find some newly-laid eggs waiting for them. The van made an ideal

Ventilation proved a great problem in the early living vans: unless a door or window was open, the men inside could be overcome by lack of oxygen quite quickly.

nesting-box, and the men who shared the summers with crafty Amos Arnold must have been pleased to have him along.[2] Other men got on less well. They grew lonely and went off to the pubs.

There was really nowhere else to go in the evenings in the villages. While the farm labourers' wives and families went to bed after the evening meal, the husbands would congregate round the pub fire to sit and talk or read the free newspapers, play games or sing songs along with a gypsy fiddler, if one should be passing through the village. When the men from the contractors' went back to the van after the pub closed they returned to an impersonal box, with no ornaments from home to cheer it up or to make it into anything more than a place to stay while the job was on. The gypsy fiddler went away to something very different.

CHAPTER 3

GYPSIES AND TINKERS

'Gypsy, gypsy, live in a tent, can't afford to pay your rent.'

Taunts like this schoolyard chant have followed the gypsies for hundreds of years. 'Egyptians' were first referred to in Britain in the sixteenth century, and they immediately aroused fear and suspicion. For a people whose main crime was to have 'no fixed abode', they attracted an extraordinary amount of ill-will. Until 1783, simply being a gypsy made an individual subject to the death penalty, and as early as 1635 a recorded secondary usage for the word was 'cunning rogue'. JPs were urged to enforce the laws in order to root out these rascals and idle beggars, 'symptomes of Popery and blynde superstition', as the Bishop of Lincoln wrote in 1622.

The authorities had very little success, and gypsies continued to roam the countryside in their tents and wagons, stopping at night in pitches for which no maps had ever been drawn but which were as well known to the travellers as the fingers on their hand. All these places had the same characteristics. There was water nearby, and a 60-foot-diameter circle of grass where the horse could graze. The ground needed to be firm and level. Mud was a great nuisance for the gypsies, who slept on the ground; moreover, if their cartwheels sank too deeply into the grass overnight the wagons would be very difficult to move in the morning.

Until the middle of the nineteenth century, all gypsies slept in tents made of bent sapling wood, probably ash or hazel, with a covering of felt or canvas or blankets. The tents came apart easily, and by day the rods were tied in bundles on either side of a horse or donkey's saddle while the covering was rolled up and carried on its back, or in the cart. Even after caravans came into use, families still had tents; the parents, perhaps with the youngest child, would sleep in the van while the other children stayed in tents pitched by the fire. Large families were considered desirable, so they could never have all crammed into the caravan together. Family duties were clearly defined. The women cooked, cleaned, did the washing and went out to find the food, while the men looked after the horses and the camp. In the morning, after a meal, the women set off to beg or read palms in the villages, or to sell whatever they

Gypsy families were usually too large to fit in the caravan all together. They needed tents as well, which were carried on the pony's back by day; these consisted of a roll of cloth, and some sapling sticks that were easy to bend over and stick into the ground.

had made in the way of mats, pegs or wickerwork. They would previously have agreed a new meeting-place for that evening. It was necessary for the men to remain behind. They could pack up and disappear in a flash if the police came, as was frequently the case, to harass the travellers.

Horses held a tremendous significance for the gypsies. Only the men worked with them. Gypsies had special rules of hygiene, which divided the world into clean and unclean objects. A horse was absolutely clean, and it would be perfectly permissible to eat from a plate that a horse had licked. A cat, on the other hand, was '*mochadi*', or ritually polluted, and if it touched a plate then that plate would have to be smashed so that no gypsy should ever eat from it again. All animals that licked their fur, and therefore took their outside dirt into their bodies, were similarly shunned. Dogs were a necessary part of life, but a gypsy always washed carefully after handling one. Each family owned at least two bowls for washing. One was used only for food, eating utensils and the tea-towels that would dry them. The other was for washing the unclean body and clothes. A gypsy would not dream of washing inside his caravan or tent, and was shocked by the idea of inside lavatories when these were installed in houses.

They preferred food that had been touched as little as possible, especially by '*gorgios*', or non-gypsies, whom they regarded as *mochadi* because of their dirty habits. A gypsy woman begging at the door would rarely accept a cup of tea for fear that an animal had touched the crockery, and because she knew it had been in a bowl in which a variety of things had been washed. Even soap was seen as a source of pollution. The food accepted was always more popular if it had first been wrapped, so the gypsy did not actually see the *gorgio* touching it. Back at home in the evening, after the meal by the fire, any leftovers were automatically thrown away because they had been handled too much to be used again. If a shadow fell across food while a gypsy was eating, this would be sufficient to taint the whole plateful, and render it *mochadi*.

All babies were born in tents on the edge of the site, because the act of birth was a potential source of pollution. Mother and child stayed on their own, eating from special plates for some weeks, and then the tent, bedding and utensils were destroyed. Women, except when past child-bearing age, were considered to be possible threats of pollution, and were expected to follow strict rules of dress and movement, never to walk in front of their men while they sat, or to step over plates of food; and to stay away from the horses.

Death took place outside the caravan as well. Gypsies had a great fear of ghosts and went to enormous lengths to make sure that the ghost or *mulo* of the dead person did not return to haunt them. The death tent was guarded, while the rest of the family or tribe sat round the fire, hoping that its light would ward off the ghost. The corpse was often dressed in inside-out clothing and placed on the shafts of his van, with the feet facing out, on the way to the graveyard. Favourite possessions and money were placed in the grave, so that the dead man would have no reason to leave his burial place. Relatives kept watch over the grave for fear of robbers, because removal of part or all of the body meant that the *mulo* could not rest.

The deceased's personal belongings were destroyed after burial. This included the van, which was burnt. The animals were either killed or sold to *gorgios*. Gypsies had a great pride in their possessions and kept them beautifully, but they could part with them without a qualm if custom so dictated. Just as they would have smashed a set of Crown Derby china if a cat had touched it, they would also automatically get rid of a dead person's crockery and furniture. If the pieces were very good, they sometimes sold them to the *gorgios*, since this amounted to the same as destroying the things themselves. If anyone kept possessions that should have been thrown away, bad luck or insanity would be expected to fall upon him, and he would be ostracized by the tribe.

Their strange customs and constant mobility made the gypsies objects of suspicion. They were suspected of stealing babies, of luring women from their happy homes, and of every theft that took place in the neighbourhood where they stopped. The fact that gypsies despised *gorgios* and regarded them as fair game when it came to selling, for example, a horse with broken wind or bishoped teeth (filed down to seem shorter so that the buyer would not realize how long in the tooth, or old, the horse really was) gave a certain justification to these feelings. This antagonism remained until the nineteenth century, when the aftermath of the Industrial Revolution encouraged a new interest in the countryside and in ancient rituals. The newly urban society felt rootless and unhappy in the filthy towns, and so people romanticized about fresh air and noble savages. The writers of the day wrote constantly about the freedom of life away from towns and factories and timetables. Percy Bysshe Shelley urged, 'Away, away from men and towns to the wild wood and the downs.' Walt Whitman wrote about the camaraderie of fellow travellers in his poem 'The Song of the Open Road'; Robert Louis Stevenson wrote, 'All I ask, the heaven above, and the road below me,' as the refrain for 'The Vagabond'. Walter Scott wrote novels that centred on life in the Middle Ages, giving the time an aura of romance and purity that fascinated a new generation of readers, including the young William Morris. George Borrow wrote *The Bible in Spain, Lavengro* and *Romany Rye* after spending a good deal of time wandering about, meeting gypsies and tinkers and living on the road himself. His books first made popular the idea that gypsies were descended from Indians. Scholars became riveted by their language and customs, and eventually a Gypsy Lore Society was formed. It published a journal which examined minutely the connections between the Romany language and Sanskrit, and the marriage rituals, tribal taboos and habits of the gypsies, whom the journal-writers believed to be pure-blooded descendants of the early nomads of India.

The popular conception of gypsies as idle vagabonds changed in response to literature. They were seen instead as 'natural' people who had found a way to live, with dignity, outside the constraints of civilized society. George Borrow in *Lavengro* gave to Jasper Petulengro, the Gypsy King, words that thrilled the romantic souls of the Victorian middle classes. 'There's night and day, brother, both sweet things; sun, moon, and stars, brother, all sweet things; there's likewise a wind on the heath. Life is very sweet, brother; who would wish to die?'

Gypsy women, especially, captured the imagination. When Bizet wrote *Carmen*,[3] he used the current perception of a female gypsy to create a character almost animal in her wilfulness, wildness and beauty. George Borrow wrote with admiration of the sorcery and devilry of the girls, and even the old women were considered lovable hags. Keats wrote, 'Old Meg she was a gypsy; And liv'd upon the moors; Her bed it was the brown heath turf, and her house was out of doors.' Later Edmund Blunden wrote, 'The gypsies lolled and gossiped, and ate their stolen swedes, Made merry with mouth-organs, worked toys with piths of reeds: The old wives puffed their pipes, nigh as black as their hair, And not one of them all seemed to know the name of care.' Even the villainess Mrs Herne in Borrow's *Lavengro*, who tried to poison the hero, was viewed with amused horror, and destined to become caught up in her own spells and prophesies.

The whole attitude of the British public to the gypsies at this time could be found in a famous rhyme written by Ralph Hodgson at the end of the century:

Time, you old Gipsy man,
Will you not stay,
Put up your caravan
Just for one day?

(There is no doubt that the Elizabethans would have turned in their graves at the sentimental tone of this verse.)

Meanwhile, the gypsies themselves continued to live as they had always done, privately, with a wary eye on the *gorgio*. If his new interest helped them in their dealings, then they were well pleased.

They did change their habits enough eventually to adapt to the caravan, although they took longer to do so than the tinkers and circus people, because they regarded themselves as a spartan group. By 1850 or '60, they were using several varieties of van, the internal layout of which had by now become fairly standard. They called the vans '*vardos*', '*vardo*' being the Romany word for wagon. Many of the different styles reflected the occupation of the owner or the particular skills of the builders. The Reading, the Ledge and the Bow Top

The Buckland caravan at Kenwood, photographed in 1964 before its restoration, is a beautiful example of gypsy van at its most ornate.

were usually favoured by gypsies, and had their wheels built so that the caravan body was slung between them. These wheels were more efficient for crossing fords, or for pulling off the road on to the rough grass verges or woodland glades. Showmen preferred the Burton van, straight-sided and with wheels that ran under the bottom of the van, allowing more living space above and running better on well-made roads. Different makers varied the interior details of their vans, and catered for clients with particular needs. Orton, Sons, & Spooner of Burton-on-Trent made mostly vans for showmen and gave their name to the type, which others also produced, to their own pattern. These vans were often very splendid and covered in highly elaborate decoration. The company also made Brush wagons, which were really shops on wheels, designed to show off the brushes, brooms, rush- and wickerwork displayed in racks and glass cases built on to the outside walls. These were the only vans with the door at the back and they had fixed steps. All the other vans had removable steps that were slung underneath the body of the caravan during travel.

The interior of the Buckland caravan shows some of the lavish fittings that were standard in the later gypsy vans.

The public had a romantic and rather sentimental conception of gypsies at the end of the nineteenth century.

Real gypsies cared little for the opinions of the gorgios. They lived their own lives by their own strict rules.

The Reading vans were built by Dunton & Sons. They lived in the perfect place for their job. By 1850, Reading was a thriving town, making a handsome living out of its position on the Bath Road, the highway from London to the West Country. It was a major stopping place for passengers, and supported many wheelwrights, harness-makers and coach-builders. Having been built on the Thames, which was used for shipping large quantities of timber, it also had a thriving industry in canvas-making and barge-building. The best Reading vans were quite exquisite, and were lighter inside than their nearest counterpart, the Bow Top, because they had windows on the side walls as well as on the back. The walls sloped outwards to allow extra space, and the interior was remarkably comfortable Inside, there was a stove on the left-hand side. Being a larger van, the Reading accommodated a bigger stove than those invented by Count Romford or the small conical-shaped Colchester stove that was known (because of its resemblance to a helmet) as the 'policeman in the corner'. Across the back end of the van ran a bed with curtains, built above drawers. On the right-hand side were seats and a chest-of-drawers. The room at night would be filled with fine silverware, best Crown Derby porcelain and snowy white linen. The bed had a good feather mattress, and the whole place was clean and shining. In the morning, all the treasures were wrapped and packed away for the day's journey.

Silvester Gordon Boswell, who was born in 1895 in Blackpool and later wrote a book about his life as a gypsy, spent his early life in a van made by Tongs of Manchester which had a Colchester stove. He remembers that there were only two gypsy vans in Blackpool at the turn of the century, and it is true that the heyday of the *vardo* was not until after 1900. The instant connection of caravans with gypsies must have owed more to the beauty and colour of the vans, and the interest in the people who travelled in them, than to the early appearance of gypsies in caravans.

There were many other people travelling around the country at the same time, and some of them were doing so in conscious imitation of the gypsies. These were gentlemen of leisure who hankered after bohemian adventures, and who were fascinated by the idea of throwing off, temporarily, the constraining values of Victorian upper-class life. In their search for excitement and new experiences they experimented with many sorts of new games and enterprises. A man called Dr William Gordon Stables, who found himself near a gypsy encampment one day and spent an idle hour wandering around the vans, was struck with the idea that he would enjoy travelling about like a gypsy. He was too fastidious to use one of their caravans, and he found the men who built the vans for travellers to be crude craftsmen who could barely read or write, although they could produce masterpieces of engineering to their own specifications. Being a well-educated Victorian, he turned in alarm from these people to the Bristol Wagon Company, a highly respectable carriage company which made railway coaches for the Great Western Railway and for export to the Empire. Dr Gordon Stables commissioned the company to build him a caravan to his own design which combined the contents of a gypsy van with some of the exterior features of a Pullman railway carriage. When it was built, he set off to see how it suited him on a series of trial rides. The first pleasure caravan was on the road.

CHAPTER 4

LEISURE AND PLEASURE

'The maintenance of health is a sacred duty. Be abstemious and sparing in the indulgence of lawful Pleasures' (*Guide to Good Health*, Dr Richter).

When Dr Gordon Stables set off down the road in his caravan to enjoy himself, he indulged in the comparatively modern activity of leisure. Holidays did not exist for most of our working ancestors, who stopped work only for religious feast days. They had no conception of pay without work, so the idea of a weekend (as opposed to just Sunday, a day of enforced inactivity) or a holiday never occurred to them. They had to take time off when they were sick, and people were terrified of illness. They tried any remedy they could find in a desperate attempt to get back into working order.

In the sixteenth and seventeenth centuries medical men put great trust in the benefits of mineral water for invalids of all kinds. This idea was not entirely new.There had been a Roman bath in the city of Bath, and a superstition that mineral water was good for health lingered on throughout the Middle Ages. The rediscovery of mineral water as a medicine encouraged towns with spas, such as Bath and Tunbridge Wells, to expand in order to accommodate the growing numbers of invalids who came to seek a cure. Rich people travelled to take the waters and would then have to spend several weeks in the vicinity in order to fill their time between sessions at the spa. By the end of the sixteenth century, exercise and relaxation were being recommended for the improvement of health, and in Bath bowling greens and a court for real tennis were installed. Travelling players, sure of an audience, came from London to entertain. Precursors of the assembly rooms, promenades and shops were built around the baths. It became such fun to be ill that rich men and women with nothing wrong with them began to mingle at the spas with the invalids.

After the Civil War, the Royalists were welcomed back from exile with open arms because they brought with them an aura of excitement that had been sadly missing during the dour and joyless years of Oliver Cromwell. The King and Queen enjoyed travelling to the spas, and the Court went with them. Ordinary people admired their exploits and came to associate watering places with glamour and high living.

The seaside and sea water took longer to catch on as a pleasurable activity. From 1700 onwards enthusiasts urged others to take cold baths, but the advantages of the sea were first made fashionable by Dr Richard Russel, a smart London doctor, in 1752. He suggested that sea water should be put to the same uses as mineral water, and once he had put the idea firmly into the heads of the liverish rich they set off eagerly to pickle their ailments in the cold waves. It is odd that sea bathing should have been invented by the British, since it must be one of the coldest places to indulge in the practice, particularly if the bather only dipped in the water and could not keep himself warm by swimming about. As the fashion grew in popularity, seaside resorts sprung up wherever they could be reached by their patrons, most of whom travelled from London. The resorts were closely modelled on the spas, and were soon patronized by the healthy and the sick alike.

By the eighteenth century, the spas were an essential part of the fashionable year, to be visited in spring and autumn, when the waters were considered most efficacious. In Bath, Beau Nash introduced strict rules to limit the numbers of people in the Assembly Rooms to a small, select group who could enjoy themselves in suitable company, and the practice of maintaining a good element of society was adopted as far as possible at all resorts.

In the same way that spas and seaside resorts deteriorated from establishments dedicated to a serious purpose to places for the pursuit of pleasure, the continental tours which had been first introduced for intellectual young gentlemen in the time of Elizabeth I had become leisure trips for tourists by the middle of the eighteenth century. The early travellers set off, chaperoned by their tutors, in order to round off their education. Travel was under strict government control, and a permit was required in order to leave the country. A young man could expect to be away from home for about three years and to undergo some danger in his wanderings. The journey was rigorous, a necessary duty, and any pleasure that resulted from it was an unexpected bonus. The European experience came to be known as the Grand Tour, and it was undertaken by larger and larger numbers of Englishmen over the next two centuries. As time passed, the educational purpose grew less important, and the cachet of having done the Tour became the purpose of the exercise. Tourists raced through country after country, providing a valuable contribution to the budding tourist industry, and barely stopped to take in the museums and galleries on the way.

In the late eighteenth century the dormeuse became popular. Fitted out with compartments for clothing, food and books, it also provided fixing places for swords and pistols. The interior could accommodate a bed if necessary, but the carriage servants would have to curl up on the rear, or rumble, seat. The owner would have used the sleeping quarters only when there was nowhere else to be found that was suitable, which might have been more often than you would think, since the British seem to have found foreign hotels very disagreeable on the whole. Diaries of the time were full of grumbles about innkeepers who overcharged for poor services and guides who failed to give proper accounts of famous battlegrounds, and there is a clear impression given that travellers returned to Britain with an enormous sigh of relief, delighted to have got the business of cultural improvement over and done with.

With the industrialization of Britain during the eighteenth and nineteenth centuries, the pattern of living altered drastically and the traditional holidays of the Church and farming calendar became less important. In the country-side employers usually knew where their workers lived, and if a man stayed away from work his employer would probably have known what his problems were and the reason for his absence. In the city, the welfare of the workers was ignored in the pursuit of profit, and the sheer numbers of people involved meant that individual circumstances were unknown to overseers at the factories. Employers claimed to believe that the working classes would not know what to do with their free time if they had any, and many genuinely thought that the Devil loved idle hands and would find easy prey amongst the poor. Pleasure, in their eyes, was only one step from depravity.

The overworked men and women felt very differently. They leapt at the chance that the newly instituted railway gave them to get away from the filth and grime of their daily surroundings. In 1841 the first excursion outing was arranged, through the Midland Counties Railway, for 510 Temperance workers to attend a delegates' meeting in Loughborough. The day was organized by Thomas Cook, who had a vision of railways opening up new horizons for the population at large. Excursions to the seaside soon became very popular and millions took advantage of the new railway routes that threaded through the low-lying coastal areas where it was easiest to build. In 1860 there were 160 million passengers, mostly heading for the beaches and spas that they associated with royalty and the fashionable set.

The Bank Holiday Act of 1871 ensured that everyone had a chance to get out for a change occasionally. Many people had never seen the sea, and they went to look at it in their droves, making the seaside resorts the fastest-growing towns in the whole of Britain for a while. The magic and romance of the water drew trippers from every corner of the land and the exclusive nature of the resorts disappeared forever.

The advantages of sea water had been extolled for centuries, and people were even persuaded to drink it for their health at times (not for long), but it was only during the second half of the nineteenth century that people began to feel that the very air that was breathed by the sea shore would do you good. Thoreau wrote, 'Fresh air is the best medicine,' and the whole country became convinced that its health depended on breathing in great gulps of it.

Until recently few had believed that they had much control over life and death. They feared disease but knew little about ways of preventing its occurrence. The poor, particularly, lived in conditions that bred disease and were unable to escape epidemics. With the trade generated by the Industrial Revolution came typhoid, cholera and other foreign scourges. When illness struck there was little to be done but pray. Doctors cost a great deal, and were not always very helpful when they came. The urban slums were as unhealthy an environment as you could find, and infant mortality remained high. Life expectancy was short, and the birth rate doubled, then doubled again at the beginning of Queen Victoria's reign as the population grew, suffered and died in the cities.

Then science stumbled on various useful discoveries. Vaccination against diseases such as diptheria, and penicillin together with a realization of the dangers of contagion and the need for cleanliness changed the odds in favour of a long and healthy life. John Wesley had said, 'Cleanliness is next to godliness,' and it became increasingly apparent that those who practised this simple dictum were protected from death and disease far more effectively than

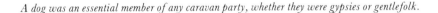

A dog was an essential member of any caravan party, whether they were gypsies or gentlefolk.

those who bought prescriptions heavily laced with addictive laudanum and alcohol. By the 1880s the birth rate had slowed down, as parents began to realize that most of their children would survive to adulthood, and that it was possible to limit their numbers if they so wished, because children were not, as they had always believed, the will of God, but the product of unprotected sex.

As late Victorian children grew up, they were taken to the seaside, they received vaccinations, and they were encouraged to exercise not only their minds but also their bodies. There was a tremendous vogue for outdoor activity, and many new sports were developed. Cricket became a national sport, seen on every village green to be the symbol of all that the Victorians held good in life. It was played in a tough but gentlemanly way, showing off the players' skill, vigour and competitive spirit to their womenfolk, who would watch appreciatively from the safety of the edge of the field, holding up their parasols against the midday sun. Golf became a mania for the well-to-do. Businessmen rushed to get home from town to Metroland (the first under-ground railway line opened in 1863) to practise their strokes for the next local tournament. Young ladies dreamed about their partners in the mixed doubles in the newly invented game of tennis. Country-house owners installed grass tennis courts which were flattened with rollers dragged by horses in special rubber shoes so that the grass remained unmarked.

The Grand Tour gravitated towards Germany and Switzerland, and above all to the mountains of the Alps. Their snowy peaks, virginal and untrampled, were an irresistible lure to young Victorian males. They clambered all over them, fascinated by the beauty of the frost and snow, and they began to make up games to play while they were there. At first skating and tobogganning were the most popular activities. The black ice on the lakes was so clear that a skater could see straight through to the fish that swam beneath. As more and more tourists arrived in Switzerland intent on enjoyment, it became desirable to make provision for them to enjoy themselves even when the vagaries of the weather thawed the natural lakes. All the resort hotels started to install ice rinks. There was a great art to this: it involved building up the layers of ice, day by day, by flooding the rink before the evening cold set in to freeze it, but not so soon that it failed to cohere to the layer of ice below. Fierce battles raged between the skaters who used two rival styles, the English and the Continental. An 'English' enthusiast was described by a Continentalist as 'diametrically opposed to every principle of nature, science and art', and similar insults were made by the other camp. In the English style, very naturally, the arms were kept by the side, and the leg unemployed by the skater at that time was held straight. The Continental skater led with his arms and used them at all possible opportunities, and always bent his unemployed leg. It was harder to skate in the English way, and Continental skating was more spectacular for the crowd to watch.

Tobogganning proved almost as popular as skating. The Cresta run was built at St Moritz in 1884 for the brave, but most people preferred an easier time. They liked evenings like one described in *Winter Sports in Switzerland* by E.F. Benson, who was a keen sportsman as well as a writer. He set off with a party from Davos, the birthplace of winter sports, on a magnificent night without a breath of wind. They travelled after dinner in a sleigh, laughing and talking all the way up to the toboggan run. They then arranged to go down at two-minute invervals, one by one. E.F. Benson was lucky enough to be last to go, and he stood for two minutes alone, without a living soul for half a mile, in the total silence of the mountains, before rushing down on his toboggan through the darkness to his friends waiting below.

Serious sportsmen took up bobbing, which got its name from the motion of leaning forward by the team, or bobbing, in order to get up speed at the start of a run. Less serious holidaymakers enjoyed ski-joring, which involved holding on to the reins of a harness while a horse pulled you along on frozen lakes or the downtrodden snow on the roads. Skiing was practised by very few people at that time. It was introduced from Norway, as a sport, by the English, and its early practitioners – men like E.C. Richardson, Vivian Caulfield, and Arnold Lunn – treated it less as a sport than a spiritual experience to which they dedicated themselves in uniforms of loose woollen socks and mittens, 'crusader' woollen caps, snow spectacles of smoked glass, windproof coats and knickerbockers. They gathered disciples, who were enthralled by the glory of skiing through the unblemished snow but were mostly scornful of the après-ski life of fancy-dress balls, concerts and ice carnivals that featured at the hotels.

Back at home in England, Dr Gordon Stables rode his pleasure caravan, the 'Wanderer', through the countryside, then wrote about his experiences, and attracted many of the people who had been out on the Alpine slopes, or on the tennis courts, to take up the sport of caravanning. At first, when the doctor travelled, he drew a good deal of attention, and was mistaken at different times for a Salvation Army general, a surgeon in attendance of a nervous lady who lurked inside the van, a travelling artist or photographer, a cheapjack, a madman, a political agitator, a king of the gypsies, or an eccentric baronet. People expressed great surprise when they discovered that he was really a retired surgeon from the Royal Navy. That they mistook him for an eccentric baronet is explained by the fact that almost immediately after the 'Wanderer' was built, several more vans were commissioned by members of the aristocracy. The 'Bohemian', built for the Duke of Newcastle by the Bristol Wagon Works, the same carriage company that made the 'Wanderer', was of a similar design but incorporated a wine cellar. The Earl of Dudley spent £450 on his caravan, a monstrosity that needed six horses to draw it along. It contained an elaborately carved chimneypiece of great weight which

Interior of the 'Wanderer': the couch in the saloon transformed into a comfortable bed at night, and the floor was covered by a fine Persian rug.

surrounded an open fire. Armchairs stood on either side, and an aviary was built into the roof. The ordinary people who lived in the villages that he passed might well have been forgiven for thinking him eccentric.

Dr Gordon Stables was an unusual character in himself. He made a good living from writing adventure stories for boys, and he wrote many books about his travels in the caravan, capitalizing on his own rather flamboyant nature and making sure that his experiences could be turned into good material for books. His book *The Cruise of the Land Yacht Wanderer*, written in 1886, described the first long journey in his caravan. The book began with a detailed record of the van, which was built from solid mahogany, with a maple interior and black and gold mouldings; its wheels and underworks were dark chocolate picked out in vermilion. The whole van was highly varnished and Dr Stables was well pleased with the effect, which he found sober and gentlemanly. The van was 20 feet long, stood 11 feet high from the ground, and had 4-foot-high hind wheels. This allowed space to carry a ladder, bucket and spade, and the framework for an after-tent, which were fixed to the vehicle's underside by day. At night a hammock could be slung underneath the van if necessary.

The interior was arranged to allow spacious accommodation. The Doctor carried a camping chair and a piano stool for spare seating, and kept in corner brackets a clock, a harmonium, a guitar, a violin, a naval sword and a good revolver. The floor was covered with lino, with a fine Persian rug on top in the saloon. The washroom contained a marble washstand, above which hung a triangular water-can, and was complete with taps. In the washroom lived the rack for plates, and pockets for towels and tea-towels. A box doubled as a chest for a valet's possessions and a seat, and there was a little flap table at which the valet could eat or read separately from his employer. At night two long, soft doormats and a cork mattress made a bed for the valet when laid (as Dr Stables put it in his beloved naval jargon) 'athwartships'. All his books were written in the kind of language that you would expect from a retired naval doctor: the caravan, for example, was always a 'land yacht' and referred to by the nautical 'she'. Generally, the attitude the writer took to his experiences gives the impression of almost a stereotype caricature of a Victorian gentleman.

Before Stables went on his travels he engaged a coachman and a valet to look after his needs. He chose Alfred Foley as his valet, a 20-year-old boy already known to him, whom he considered suitable because he read 'the Book', had a religious mother, did not flirt with maids at the inns, could be trusted with the dog, and did not snore. The coachman was procured through an advertisement in the *Reading Mercury*, and was hired after presenting references from an army major. Dr Stables, not averse to a drop himself, was very concerned to know that his coachman was temperate, and decided to hire John G. because the man was quiet and polite and thoroughly knew his place. The fact that he was fond of horses was the last qualification that Dr Stables found worthy of mention.

Also travelling with the party was a parrot called Polly, who was white with a crimson garland on her chest and blue patches round her eyes. She was five years old and had belonged to the doctor for a year. A sulky creature as a rule, she changed utterly when she heard a guitar playing, and immediately began to beat time on the bars of her cage. When she listened to the violin, she raised one foot in the air and stood with downcast head as she slowly opened and shut her fist in time to the music. She particularly admired a melancholy air.

With typical Victorian sentimentality, the place of honour in the caravan was reserved for the dog, a champion black-haired Newfoundland called Hurricane Bob. This dog slept in the van with his master even though, unlike the valet, he snored at times. He had a reputation for fighting, but Dr Stables indulgently forgave him for the habit, since he never touched small dogs and was therefore a good sporting fellow.

Dr Gordon Stables was a hard task-master. His valet, Foley, who sits in his own tent for the photograph, would rarely have had time to rest between chores while the van was on tour.

Soon after setting off on his wanderings, Gordon Stables recorded in his journal the details of a typical day as a gentleman gypsy. The morning began at 6 o'clock, when Foley the valet would wake the doctor for his daily bath, having first erected the after-tent where the ablutions took place. The coachman, who always slept in a nearby inn so that he could keep an eye on the two horses in the stables, arrived to collect oats for them from the bucket kept slung beneath the caravan. Stables and Foley always slept in the van, Stables because it was his pleasure, and Foley in order to fulfil his duties. While the bath was in progress the valet shook and folded the sheets outside in the fresh air, then rearranged and dusted the saloon. He then spread a cloth on the folding table and laid up for breakfast. The Doctor emerged from under his tent, invigorated by his cold-water wash squeezed from a huge sponge that had been dunked in a bucket, and whistled to Hurricane Bob before setting off for a brisk early-morning stroll. He returned to a breakfast of bacon and eggs cooked by Foley on an oil-stove, in a tent made of mats underneath the caravan.

After the washing-up had been completed, by Foley of course, the caravan set off, with Dr Stables supervising the tricky manoeuvre of getting out of the meadow through a farm gate that was usually only just wider than the 6-foot 8-inch caravan. Once 'she' was safely on the road, her master retired into the saloon to read the paper while John drove, and Foley cycled a hundred yards ahead on the Ranelagh Club tricycle that was part of the equipment for the journey. At 10 o'clock John the coachman drew up on the verge. Dr Stables was hungry again after inhaling so much fresh country air, and ate a hearty lunch of cold roast beef and floury new potatoes, accompanied by a salad, while John tended to the horses at a nearby inn. While he waited for his lunch to come, the Doctor wrote his log for the day. When the party set off once more Dr Stables retired into the van to snooze until a suitable meadow by an inn was found for the evening camp. Then he went for a spin on the tricycle while Foley made the beds up for the night and cooked the supper. The coachman made his way to the inn, the valet put up the shutters and disappeared to his cubbyhole and his cork mattress, while Dr Stables read in bed or wrote until he sank into a deep and healthy sleep before 11 o'clock. Despite his rigorous schedule Foley never rebelled against the hard work required of him on those journeys, and if the book is to be believed, he never in fact felt anything but respect and admiration for his master.

The direction of the Wanderer's maiden voyage was decided in the beginning by the tossing of a pebble. It twice landed pointing towards the north-west, so the caravan set off for Reading and parts north. When it reached Durham Dr Stables observed the miners and their families from the safety of his van; he thought them dirty and drunken, fond of gambling and probably child-batterers; the men were likely to shove old ladies out of their way. He mused in his journal when he passed through a village called Three Mile Bridge: 'It is quite a mineing place [*sic*] far from wholesome, but the children looked healthy, a fact which is due, doubtless, to the bracing pure air they breathe. All are bare-legged and shoeless, from the lad or lass of fifteen down to the month-old kicking baby.'

Soon afterwards he found, when climbing the hills of Northumbria, that it was very hard for the horses to stagger to the crest of the hills without slipping backwards. He stopped at one point, on a steep incline near the gate of the castle of Alnwick, the ancient home of the Percys, in order to admire the view, and then found that the horses were unable to gather enough momentum to finish the climb to the top of the hill. They staggered and clawed at the road, then started to go backwards. The roller, which all caravans carry for such emergencies, was placed behind one of the back wheels, but would not have been sufficient to halt the backward slide without a huge stone that was shoved behind the other wheel just in time to stop an awful accident. Within a very short time, twelve sturdy Northumbrians appeared out of the countryside and put their shoulders to the van, until it was pushed to the top of the hill. If their kind behaviour altered Dr Stables' view of the men of that neighbourhood at all, he did not see fit to remark upon it in his journal, and he probably accepted their help as his natural due in the order of things.

Further along the road the caravan passed a large number of vans and wagons going in the opposite direction to the fair at Falkirk. The coachman declared that he was glad that they were going the other way, and the doctor added that 'however pleasant it may be to wave a friendly hand or to exchange a kindly word or smile with these "honest" gypsies, it is not so nice to form a part in a Romany Rye procession.' He then went on to describe in a lyrical way the different vans, 'some all paint and gold, some dingy as smoke. All happy, all smiling, all perspiring.' He was happy to share the romantic view of gypsies that his generation approved, but horrified at the idea that he might have been mistaken for a member of their ranks in any serious way.

This fear never troubled a fellow gentleman gypsy of the time. George Bankes was an amiable Old Etonian who would not have given two figs for what the man in the street thought about him. He set off in high spirits for a journey from Bordeaux to Genoa, in November 1889, in a gypsy caravan with red wheels called the 'Escargot' that measured 13 feet long and 6 foot 6 inches from floor to ceiling. With him went his wife Peggy and their collie James. Peggy was a good sort who battled bravely with the unfamiliar tasks of caravan life. In George's book about the adventure, *Across France in a Caravan*, he describes the kitting out of the van, with the usual accoutrements of tobacco jar, pipe-rack and revolver, and adds that Peggy made the whole seem more homely by pinning photos and fans to the walls, and placing on the bed a counterpane made in her ancestral tartan.

51

The caravan and the collie went to Bordeaux from St Katherine's wharf in London on the good ship *Albatross*, while George and Peggy hurried ahead to get all the paperwork and customs formalities sorted out. They bought two horses and secured a certificate of respectability from the Préfet of Bordeaux on the advice of French friends who warned them that if they could only produce British passports when challenged by the gendarmerie on the roads they would be in imminent danger of arrest. When the van arrived, the two horses that George had bought proved to be absolute duds who would only back up when attached to the shafts of a wagon. This rather embarrassed George, in very much the same way that the rash purchase of a clapped-out sports car might today, a hundred years later, bother a young man.

This was to be the first of a string of disasters. When Peggy attempted to cook a meal on their first day in the van she managed to smoke out the living quarters so disastrously during the preparation of an omelette and cutlets that the couple immediately decided to hire a boy to help with the daily chores.

When they finally got under way, pulled by a sulky and lazy horse called Missus and her cheerful partner Mary Ann, they took with them a young man called Joseph, who proved himself invaluable from the start. He dug them out of muddy ruts, found tracer ponies to help pull them up the hills, dealt with the difficulties at bridges and wayside halts, and did all the shopping (because he was French he was not cheated in the markets as they would have been). He was good with the horses when they caught colds in the incessantly rainy weather and helped to maintain a feeling of optimism. The money often ran short between towns where drafts had been arranged with banks. It was hard to obtain credit from disbelieving officials, even with a letter of respectability, when the travelling address was 'the Escargot'. On New Year's Day 1890, Peggy had neuralgia, even Joseph was ill, and one of the horses had a badly swollen leg. It rained all day.

With true Victorian grit, the couple struggled on, creeping up hills and careening down the other side. Peggy got over her neuralgia, bought some sabots and became more attuned to the French landscape. George never failed to be cheerful. He even managed to see the joke when they came back to the van one day to find a pie that Peggy had made for them with enormous effort, and left wrapped for protection in a copy of the *Petit Journal* while they went out, was now covered in the news of the day, which had transferred itself on to the pie's pastry roof. When they met other travellers they were unfailingly friendly to them. They were delighted when a caravan containing a husband and sad-looking wife, who were '*joueurs de Comédie*', drew up beside them; the couple's intention was to try to make a bargain with Bankes and company to refrain from performing in certain of the cafés in town! They also met and made friends with an English giant who travelled in a freak show and claimed to be an old Grenadier Guard. On closer questioning, he admitted that he had never been in the Guards but had come from Market Drayton in Shropshire, where his father was an unsuccessful farmer who had died in debt. The young giant had accepted a job in Wombwell's circus to pay off the debts, but he hated the life. Like those of so many over-tall men, his joints were weak and he could not work normally. He had a wife and children to support, so he continued, reluctantly, to earn a livelihood by exploiting his disability. He travelled with his wife in a specially-made caravan which was wide enough to accommodate his 8-foot-tall body.

Another sad giant appears in one of several books of fiction that were written about caravanning at the turn of the century. In *The Slowcoach*, a book for children by E.V. Lucas, a young family is given a caravan by an unknown friend, who has it delivered with an anonymous note one afternoon. It is a

Dr Gordon Stables was the first gentleman to take up caravanning, and his van the 'Wanderer',
which he called his 'land yacht', caused great curiosity among villagers as he travelled along –
accompanied by a valet, a coachman, a Newfoundland dog and a bad-tempered parrot.

gypsy van with a green body, blue panels and white blinds with red sashes. The note tells the children that the van has previously belonged to a lady artist and not to gypsies, so they are not to worry about its cleanliness. 'This is the right kind of caravan,' the note continues. 'The brown caravans, highly varnished, are wrong: they may be more luxurious, but no gypsy would look at them.' The vans referred to were the type resembling Dr Stables' 'Wanderer' or the Duke of Newcastle's 'Bohemian'. It is interesting that the author suffered from the same confusion of attitude towards gypsies that affected Gordon Stables. He was drawn to the idea of the authentic and picturesque *vardo*, but was careful to make it clear that the real gypsies had never touched or tainted the caravan he wrote about.

The story takes the children into a series of adventures on the road, where they meet typical wayfarers of the period. An artist living in a caravan gives them some useful practical tips for the travelling life, such as tying a fern to the horse's head to keep off flies, or shoving a cabbage-leaf under their hats to ward off the heat of the midday sun. A wicked old Irish tinkerwoman robs them, some gypsies give them a couple of rabbits – which they eat at once in case they proved to have been poached – and they meet the Human Colossus, a giant who hates his work in the circus and has to share his van with a spiteful dwarf called King Pip. They suffer the indignity, common to many caravanners in novels of the period, of disappearing into a cloud of dust as a newfangled motor-car roars past them, scattering mayhem in its wake.

Toad, from Kenneth Grahame's *Wind in the Willows*, is probably the most famous character of all time to have ridden in a caravan. When his smartly painted canary yellow *vardo* is passed by a 'magnificent motor-car, immense, breath-snatching, passionate, with its pilot tense and hugging his wheel', Toad, who is notorious for his fickle habit of moving from fad to fad in a most Victorian way, drops his interest in the caravan and gazes lovingly into the distance at the vanishing car, murmuring 'poop-poop' to himself in a daze of admiration. Not so his companion Rat, who sees the horse rear, plunge back up and turn the van into the ditch, smashing its little red wheels into smithereens. He shouts, 'You road hog!' at the disappearing speck of dust, and in doing so echoes the words of many real-life caravanners who had developed a loathing for the imperious honking, noise and brashness of the motor-car.

Before he switches his affection to cars, Toad runs true to form in other respects as a typical gentleman gypsy. He loves the idea of the freedom to roam and the doll's-house quality of the little bunks, tables and cupboards for food, baccy, soda water, cards and dominoes; but he has no intention of mucking in with the work involved with life away from home and servants. On the first night out in the van with Rat and Mole, he eats a meal with them under the stars, sitting on the grass, then goes to bed saying, 'Goodnight, you

*Villagers thought gentlemen gypsies like the Duke of Newcastle in his van the 'Bohemian' were
quite mad when they saw them trundling by, loaded with all the comforts of home, on the open road.*

fellows. This is the real life for a gentleman.' In the morning he is so heavily
asleep that by the time he gets up Rat and Mole have made the fire, washed
up from the night before, fetched eggs and milk from the village and cleaned
the van. When the next stop comes, and Toad is firmly told to help with the
chores, he seems far less enthusiastic about the whole venture. 'Travel,
change, interest, excitement' are all he craves. He leaves the humdrum
necessities of everyday life to lesser mortals.

In *The Caravaners* (*sic*), by Mary Annette Von Arnim, the author pokes fun
at a character very similar to Toad, a German baron called Otto who finds
himself embarked upon a caravan holiday in Kent with his wife, his two
glamorous German sisters (one of whom is married to an Englishman), a
socialist MP and a young man studying for the Church. The Baron hates the
uncomfortable accommodation, cannot fathom the social niceties of the
English, is stuffy, conceited, class-ridden and pompous, and is used as a
catalyst in the story. This centres on the attitude of this group of upper-class
bohemians, who adopt gypsy clothes (to the Baron's disgust) and sit around
discussing artists and writers and agonizing over the best way to improve the

lot of the people who live on their estates. They pride themselves on their liberal views and scoff at the conventions of the Baron, but even this enlightened group takes two hours between them to produce eggs and coffee of indifferent quality on their first night together, and great tensions develop over the question of washing-up and cleaning rotas.

Cooking, cleaning, managing the horses and living outside the rules were the great novelties for the gentleman gypsy and his sisters. They were unusual enough to have given the time they spent in caravans a truly bohemian flavour, but they were also the activities that palled most quickly. For many people in this new age of leisure, the reality of 'slumming it' was often less amusing than expected and the craze for a caravan easily faded after a few weeks spent rattling and banging through summer lanes. The meals tasted wonderful, the sleep was profound, the air brought roses back into the cheeks, and the company on the road had the thrill of novelty, but the sheer pleasure had to be balanced against the tedious and mundane nature of everyday chores. It was easy to shrug and turn from caravanning to the next amusement on offer when the going got rough unless there was a specific purpose to living in a van. Those with a reason, a mission or a cause which could be helped by travelling on the road were prepared to put up with a certain amount of discomfort on the way, but the pleasure-seekers only stayed long enough to enjoy themselves, never after the experience had ceased to be fun.

CHAPTER 5

MEN WITH A MISSION

The explorer Sir Samuel Baker chose a caravan as his means of transport in Cyprus in 1879 not because of any romantic associations but because it was the most practical way of getting around an island where the main roads were no better than donkey tracks. Baker went to Cyprus to look over the newly occupied island and assess its possible uses for the British government. He was in his late fifties when he set off, and he took his wife with him, so he felt that he was entitled to a measure of comfort on the way, which a caravan would provide. Sir Samuel and his wife were both redoubtable travellers who had endured far greater privations in the past on their trips to the African interior, moving on horseback or by foot for months at a time.

Sir Samuel Baker was one of a group of restless Victorians who were all bent on solving one of the great mysteries of the nineteenth century. The exact location of the source of the Nile was an obsession to the British at that time, and the glory that awaited the first man to confirm its whereabouts attracted the most adventurous spirits of the generation. In 1856 Richard Burton and John Speke penetrated into the interior from Zanzibar. They came back to England with differing theories as to the meaning of the sights they had seen, and Speke set off again with a new partner called Captain James Grant in search of further proof to show that Lake Victoria was the indisputable source of the Nile.

Men who went to Africa disappeared into the jungle, and were often *incommunicado* for years at a time, as if dead, until they suddenly re-emerged from the undergrowth. Riddled with fever, their entourage reduced from the original army of servants and equipment to a few loyal bearers, they staggered blinking into the light bringing with them news of wild tribes and bloody rituals, together with confusing descriptions of seminal lakes and their tributaries. More dead than alive, they arrived to a hero's welcome in England, which often degenerated amid a welter of squabbles with the other returned explorers. They bickered over the findings of their years of tribulation in the realms of darkness so fiercely that they felt compelled to go back to Africa and its horrors to justify their honour.

When Speke and Grant failed to return after an exceptionally long time from their African expedition, Sir Samuel Baker, who in any case knew Speke personally, felt moved to go and look for them. He organized the expedition out of his own pocket (other travellers usually went under the auspices of the Royal Geographical Society) and set off for the Nile taking his newly acquired and glamorous young Hungarian wife along with him. After failing to contact Speke and Grant, he branched off by camel across the Nubian desert and wandered near to the Blue Nile for the next twelve months. The countryside there was all that Baker could wish for. He had already built up a reputation as a superlative hunter. His exploits with a gun were famous. One story, told of him when he lived in Ceylon, claimed that when cornered by a wounded bull buffalo he used up the last of his ammunition, then took the coins from his pocket and loaded his gun with them. As the beast charged, he fired 'three shillings' worth of small change' at the buffalo's head and stunned it sufficiently to allow him time to escape. He enjoyed danger and sport, and hunted for pleasure rather than gain. This astonished the natives that he met, whose only contact with white men until then had been the traders who came to the interior for one of two reasons: they wanted ivory, or they wanted slaves, and they did not care what methods they used in pursuit of their quarry.

When the Bakers finally came back to Khartoum in 1862, they found that Speke and Grant were still unaccounted for. They travelled up the Nile once more as far as Gordokov in the hope of hearing news, and unexpectedly witnessed their arrival from the jungle almost immediately. Baker was slightly piqued to hear from the jubilant pair that they had discovered the source of the Nile without any shadow of a doubt, but he was glad that they had come out alive to tell the tale, so he put a brave face on his disappointment. He resolved to go and explore the lake they had found, and add to their knowledge of the geography of the region. After many adventures – Lady Baker nearly died from sunstroke, and her honour came under threat when the capricious King Kamrasi suggested a wife-swap with Sir Samuel (a proposition which he countered by pointing a gun at the king's heart while the court gazed on in stunned amazement) – the couple drank from the waters of Lake Albert Nyanza before travelling home to emerge in their turn, like skeletons, into the glare of civilization and acclaim.

They returned to the area some years later, hired by the corrupt Khedive of Egypt to take control of the land on the banks of the Nile. They were lured by the Khedive's stated desire that he wanted Sir Samuel to take the job so that he could stamp out the slave trade in the region. Although the Khedive's motives may in reality have been less than noble, the British at any rate were becoming increasingly restive about slaves. Some churchmen and politicians had spoken out against the practice for many years; gradually the public too, became aware of the real horrors of the trade, and pressed for abolition. In 1848, Samuel Wilberforce gave a speech in the House of Lords in which he declared that 'cheap sugar means cheap slaves', and pleaded passionately against the importation of slave-picked sugar on the same terms as free labour produce. The churches collected money and sent out missionaries to Africa. Most of them died of fever, but as each one succumbed another stood ready to take his or her place. Like the explorers, they showed extraordinary courage, driven on by their uniquely Victorian sense of duty.

This moral sense, which made the British feel responsible for the welfare of their less fortunate brethren, was accompanied by an arrogance that suffered a few knocks in the year that Samuel Baker went to Cyprus in his caravan. There was a war in Afghanistan against a stubborn and intractable army. Soon after Baker landed in Larnaca, a simultaneous war in South Africa reached a disastrous stage when the Zulus wiped out a battalion of three hundred men at Rorke's Drift. Britain was stunned with grief by the news of

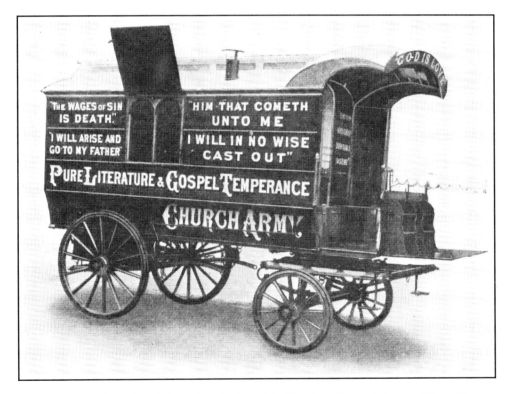

Often several vans from different denominations of the Church would turn up, in competition with each other, at public events.

the massacre, and badly needed more cheerful reports from the third theatre of its military operations, the recently occupied island of Cyprus.

The Bakers arrived with their van, which unlike those of other gentlemen gypsies of the period had actually been purchased from the gypsies. Having been exposed to smallpox in Africa and the miasmas of the Nile, they were probably less finicky than less cosmopolitan caravanners. Their 'hut on wheels' was small, only 9 foot 6 inches long and 5 foot 8 inches wide. It contained a permanent bed, with a chest-of-drawers beneath, that was built of American walnut, a superb wood that did not shrink. There was also a table and lockers for crockery. The stove had been taken out altogether, and the chimney was replaced by a ventilator. As an added feature, the Bakers brought along a large open-brasswork Egyptian lantern with glass of various colours that burned candles and warmed the caravan at night. They considered it very splendid, but it was too bright and everyone banged their heads on it all day long, so it was eventually abandoned. Following the gypsy caravan came another van, which contained the luggage and was fitted with a sliding deck formed of movable planks. This slotted into place 2 foot 6 inches from the roof and formed sleeping berths for the servants. Both vehicles had thick, broad iron wheels which projected out $5/8$ inch on either side of the felloes to provide a wide surface for crossing deep soil or sandy ground.

When the van arrived in Cyprus it aroused a lot of interest, and Sir Samuel himself caught one small boy wriggling in through a window. His toes had made the first marks on the virgin varnish of the van and Baker regretted that he had no stick with which to thrash the boy. Once delivered, the van was too big to progress down the main street. After it had finally been manhandled to Craddock's Hotel it had suffered considerable damage. A local blacksmith repaired it and at the same time modified the design by adding a bullock pole between the shafts so that it could be drawn by oxen instead of horses, which tended to be small and weak in Cyprus. Two beautiful pairs were hired, along with their drivers and all expenses for fodder, for the sum of 12 shillings a day.

At the time that the party left Larnaca it included Amarn, an Abyssinian servant who had been with Sir Samuel since he was hired as a 9-year-old boy in Africa, a Greek cook called Christo, and a big, handsome, lazy man called Georgi, who had turned up at the hotel in rags in search of work. Baker liked his face, and took him on. He felt rather pleased with himself for risking such a thing, knowing that most of his compatriots would never have considered such a disreputable-looking figure. He arranged for a suit of clothes to be made up to match those worn by Amarn. These consisted of a tunic, waistcoat, knickerbockers and garters, of navy blue serge. After Georgi had submitted to a haircut and donned his servants' uniform he appeared respectable enough to take up his place on the caravan. Three spaniels, Merry, Shot and Wise, completed the group, and were at once put to work by

Sir Samuel, who shot enough larks on the first day out to make a pilaff.

Baker's impression of Cyprus was on the whole unfavourable. He found the women ugly and slovenly in dress, and at one point was so moved by disgust of them and their flea-bitten necks that he hazarded a guess that they were living proof of a curse put on their famous ancestress, Venus, in revenge for her over-abundance of beauty. The land looked to him like a desert, with stretches of thistles growing in the chalky ground for miles on end.

Despite the traveller's poor opinion of their country, the people of Cyprus were friendly, and always handed sweet herbs or flower bunches to Lady Baker when the caravan passed through their villages. When the van jammed in the main street of a small town called Dali, an old woman came and held burning olive leaves under the nostrils of the oxen to avert the evil eye while young women scattered orange-flower water over Sir Samuel and his wife as a sign of welcome. A crowd of men pushed the van from behind while others sawed off the wooden water spouts that stuck out from their houses into the street so that the van could pass. Others dug up paving stones that barred the way. The Bakers took this generous attention as their right; unmoved by the people's kindness, Sir Samuel continued to pour scorn on the old hags of women, whom he 'found painful to look upon'. He only recovered his good humour with the island when he reached Famagusta.

Here he discovered a great natural harbour, easily fortifiable and impressive enough to make Cyprus valuable to the British. He was fascinated by the deserted fort there, and often walked through the desolation and rubble left by the sack of the Turks in 1571, which still lay scattered while 'the filth of ages sweltered among these blood-sodden ruins'.

He was quick to note that the Turkish influence could be seen in the women, whom he found a superior breed to their swarthy neighbours. Delicate hands, clean clothes and pretty faces could be seen amongst the orange and olive groves around Kyrenia. The Bakers abandoned their caravan to stay at a monastery in Trooditissa while Sir Samuel wrote his report of the journey. He concluded that Cyprus needed no troops to control the peaceful natives, that the terrain was suited to the growing of cotton or silk, that the water was good, and that since consumption was unknown (the Cypriots did not drink from cows but preferred goat or sheep milk) and dysentery rarely occurred, it was a good place for invalids to come to recuperate in the months between October and May.

At the time when Sir Samuel Baker's attention was fixed on the Nile and the scourge of slavery, the Church of England was intent on the formation of foreign missions, but as the years passed it became increasingly aware of the misery on its own doorstep. The pity aroused by the plight of starving Africans dragged from their loved ones and forced to work long, punishing hours for foreign masters was easily deflected on to the shame of dying

The young men travelling in the Salvation Army 'forts' slept on mattresses made of seaweed wrapped in American leather.

children in the British mills, whose working conditions were no better than those of the slaves. As the churchmen began to feel sympathy for their own less fortunate brethren stirring in their souls, an evangelical attitude grew in strength, both in the established Church and in newly found movements such as General William Booth's Christian Mission, later to be known as the Salvation Army.

Clergymen, fostered by the evangelical 'Palmerston Bishops', tried to improve the conditions of the poor by opening night schools for adult education, forming workmen's institutes and holding mothers' meetings. They encouraged women to have a much more positive role in parish work, even to the extent in the case of a leading Church of England evangelist, the Reverend William Pennefather, of organizing a home for deaconesses, who could wear a shared form of uniform, live together and devote their lives to good works amongst the poor. The Reverend Pennefather was a good example of the evangelists of the mid-nineteenth century. Well-born, shocked by the poverty that he saw during the 1846 potato famine in Ireland where he was abysmally helpless in his desire to save both Protestants and Catholics from their misery, he became increasingly involved in the social problems of his parishioners as well as in their spiritual needs. In the hope of attracting more working men to his services, he converted an old boat by the wharf in one of his parishes into a floating chapel. He spent a great deal of time working at the fair which came to his part of Barnet every August and where he saw the livelihoods of the travelling showmen begin to disappear as the hiring fairs dwindled in importance. He eventually set up an annual conference at his last parish, Mildmay Park, and evangelists from around the world came there to meet and exchange ideas. His biographer, the Reverend Robert Braithwaite, was proud to report that he shared his dinner-table with a coloured man. 'Dear Pennefather's table was open to all the people of God alike,' he wrote. He also encouraged temperance workers to speak in public. One of the main features of the evangelist movement was its abhorrence of alcohol and the evils attendant upon it. By 1872, although the Reverend Pennefather had already died, the Mildmay conference was an important enough event to attract as a speaker the famous American evangelist, Dwight Moody, who then returned a year later with his collaborator, Ira Sankey, to make a triumphant tour of Britain, drawing huge crowds and gathering enormous amounts in the collection boxes. Moody's stories reduced many of the congregation to tears, and Ira Sankey was blessed with a singing voice that thrilled his listeners to the soul. They and their contemporary Philip Phillips, who started his career as a religious singer by riding around New England in a caravan, were successful men who worked for the Lord to an organized schedule and lived in comfortable prosperity.

The rank and file of the evangelist movement had a much harder time. In

1885 the Salvation Army, which had been sending out its soldiers for the last twenty years, hit upon the idea of mobilizing a Cavalry Corps, which would travel in a movable camp, or fort, so that groups could go around the country to sell the magazine *War Cry*, and preach in the villages where there was no established Salvation Army 'depot'. These 'forts' were in fact caravans, custom-made by the Bristol Wagon Works Company. Designed to hold thirteen people, they were quite large: 18 feet in length and 8 feet wide. They stood 9 feet 4 inches high, but despite their bulk they were light enough to be pulled by two horses, thanks to the skill the Bristol Wagon Works company had developed from its now considerable experience in the caravan trade. The front of the fort was constructed so that it could double as a platform for the holding of open-air meetings on village greens, and at the rear of this platform was a space 6 feet 6 inches by 4 feet which held a washstand on one side and a small cooking stove on the other. This could be partitioned off from the interior of the van by a sliding door or left open in winter to allow the stove to act as a heater. Ample provision was made for ventilation, a necessary precaution for a dormitory full of thirteen young men and their officer, all sleeping heavily after a day spent trudging many miles to sell a few copies of *War Cry* before hurrying back for an open-air meeting in the evening.

Each man in the fort was issued with a knapsack for comb, toothbrush, clothes-brush, Bible, hymn book and copies of *War Cry*. These were based on the design used for the Queen's Army. In the caravan every man was allowed a single and a double blanket and a box for his personal bits and pieces, to be kept under one of the lower bunks. The mattresses were made of seaweed covered in American leather, and the pillows were of the same material. Life was hard, and the reception in the villages varied enormously from one place to another. The young men were often pelted with stones, flour or eggs, but they relied almost entirely for their needs to be supplied by the kindness of the people who lived near their camping sites; somehow the gifts of food always materialized and the men ate, through various generous donations that often came from the poorest members of the community. The vans bore names such as 'Rescue', 'Conqueror', 'Mercy' and 'Deliverer'. They set off after dedication services held either at the Congress Hall in Clapton or at provincial meeting-places. *War Cry* reported that the 'Deliverer' was dedicated at a 'red-hot' meeting in Rochdale. On the journey from London to Lancashire the fort travelled from ten to twenty miles each day with the men tramping through mud, rain, snow and frost.

The first winters on the road were very tough. An official who was detailed to visit the training depot at Burford only realized while he rode towards it in a trap from the station that the depot was not a house, but the caravan 'Conqueror', which was parked in a yard just outside the village surrounded by snow-covered fields. The van door opened and light streamed out as the lads ran to welcome the visitor and take him indoors. When he asked how they managed to live in such conditions, the Captain of the depot replied:

Oh, the van's comfortable enough. Trouble is, it's too comfortable. When we're all in at dinner and the door shut and the fire in, it's so warm we feel the cold terribly when we turn out to visit. Nights, it's cold of course. The blankets freeze into the windows regularly but we're used to that. The first night it didn't look so cheerful. It was a regular downpour and our lamps went out and we'd only a bit of bread and cheese. But once we got to work, it was glorious.

The officer left full of praise for their work but undoubtedly glad to get back on the train on his way to warmth and civilization.

There were compensations. In summer, the caravans took on an almost holiday atmosphere at times. Another officer, sent to spend a Sunday with the troops in the field, this time with a 'lasses' ' cavalry fort at Ickleford, reported on the day in *War Cry* with great enthusiasm. The 'Victory' stood in a farmyard, looking homely and picturesque. Smoke came from the chimney, and everyone sat around chattering over mugs of tea, or eating food from the generous stock that had been donated by the villagers. The walk from the caravan to the meeting through the night breeze at the end of the day, under a floating banner, completed the picture of summer fun.

Once a barracks was established in a village and had a regular room or hall set up as a meeting-place, the caravan forts moved on to the next town picked as a target for salvation. In 1891 a young cadet called William Henderson wrote a description in his diary of his time as a member of the Corps sent to open up Chesham. He was proud of the van, the 'Integrity', and noted that it was larger and better than the caravans that they met on the road from time to time. He liked the paintwork, of army blue below and red on top, with its two crests and the name of the fort written on either side. The Blood and Fire flag fluttered above the round ventilators set into the edge of the roof to lighten the interior, and the whole effect looked very smart. As a cadet, or 'candidate', he was expected to perform certain tasks in the caravan according to a weekly rota. Working in pairs, the boys either cleaned all the boots, folded blankets, cooked the meals or examined the lamps and checked if they needed oil before cleaning the glass.

William Henderson enjoyed most of his time in the 'Integrity', although he was upset when people he met stayed aloof or rejected him. When they first arrived in town, the fort members found a camping site on a muddy bit of land at the far end of Chesham, and the boys on boot duty dreaded the daily round of cleaning. It was a cold, wet May and the first meetings were held in a barn that was swarming with rats, draughty and discouraging. After a while things improved, and William listed the range of gifts brought to the 'Integrity' by outsiders: sides of bacon, rounds of beef, meat pies, dumplings,

The van hired to tour the summer fairs was so successful that a custom-made caravan was built for the St Andrew's Mission.

Many missionaries carried a harmonium, and held services, inside their vans. They hoped to persuade people to take 'the pledge' – that is, to give up alcohol.

puddings, tarts, gooseberries, apples, jam, tea and sugar. When the fort left town after five months William wrote, 'Glory to God, we can say that we left the town better than what we found it.' He recorded the great sorrow of the townspeople at their departure, all of whom wished that the fort could remain forever. Judging from the diary – the writer of which cheerfully accepts the possibility of a dousing on the doorstep with a bucket of water from time to time, gives genuine thanks for the gift from a little girl of a pound of sugar and 2½ pence, and follows the accounts of bad times, honestly recorded, with a self-reminder that they 'do it all for the Lord and He makes it all right' – the people of Chesham, Bucks, whatever their feelings may have been about the Salvation Army in general, may well have been sorry to lose the company of a thoroughly nice boy.

The Army was not the only religious group in Britain at the time to travel the roads with caravans. There were many, often turning up at the same events at once. In *A Parish on Wheels*, the Reverend Howard Swinstead, who travelled around the fairs in a caravan under the auspices of the Bishop of Salisbury, told a story of an over-abundance of preachers. He had camped in a fairground ready for work amongst the travellers the next day, and in the morning he was joined by a Church Army colporteur, which pulled up near him, its keeper ready to sell books to all comers and to exchange pious words with the public. At noon, a queer-looking van, which the Reverend Swinstead nicknamed the 'Pill-box', also appeared, carrying a man who claimed that the whole world was his parish. His stock included works that offered an 'easy and cheap shortcut to the celestial kingdom'. The Reverend Swinstead accepted a book that the man presented to him and was rather annoyed that the one he offered in return was refused out of hand. He suggested that since the entire world constituted this man's parish, perhaps he could move on to another part of it, as this piece was already quite well covered in the religious sense. The man departed; in the evening the Reverend Swinstead combined forces with the preacher from the Church Army and with the local parish clergy to hold a service in the open air with them: 'For half an hour, the swing-boats and coconut balls stopped their motion and van-dwellers and parishioners all joined together in most brotherly harmony.'

The Reverend Howard Swinstead was very different in character and background to the men who manned the Salvation Army forts. Well educated and well connected, he approached the people amongst whom he worked from an intellectual and paternal viewpoint and took a particular interest in the gypsies and travelling people who went round from fair to fair. He was intrigued by their habits, and carefully noted their ways when he visited them in his position as a peripatetic clergyman, on call to go wherever death, trouble or disease required immediate help. For seven months of the year, from 5 April to 6 November, he travelled, baptizing babies on the tailboards of caravans, giving slide shows and talks, holding services in the open and trying to set up some form of schooling for the children. Gypsy children had no education, and most gypsies could neither read nor write. The children were often turned away if they attempted to attend the local schools in the town where they stopped. The Reverend Swinstead did what he could to change the situation, so that by presenting a card at each place they arrived on their travels the children could attend lessons and acquire the rudiments of education.

At first the Reverend Swinstead travelled in a hired van, taken for a nine-week trial period to test the usefulness of staying amongst his parishioners on the road. The van had formerly belonged to a political agitator, and when it appeared in villages people often shouted out, 'What's yer colour?' assuming that the van carried politicians. 'Black and white,' was the clergyman's quick response; 'Read it.' Then a tract was handed down. During the first summer with the hired van, meetings were usually held in barns and sheds, but after that the diocese funded the St Andrew's Mission with its own custom-made caravan, which boasted an extending piece to the front of the roof. This made an excellent sounding-board, under which the missioner could preach or from which he could hang a 6-foot-square sheet like a roller blind, that was then pegged at the bottom to the turf by means of two forks and string. After slides had been shown on it and the sheet carefully re-folded, the same extension could be fitted with a canvas cover so that the area formed a compartment for the servant to sleep on a hammock. In the morning, it converted into a bathroom, with an india-rubber bath which could be erected in a trice. The van was 13 feet long and 6 foot 6 inches wide, and measured 7 feet from floor to ceiling. Four of the side panels were on hinges and could be opened on one side to show eight divisions, each furnished with a bright selection of books and picture cards for sale to the public, and to be handed out as gifts to the travellers who could 'read a dear little bit'. Above the bookshop was a picture describing the weekly paper *Sunday* in glowing terms. The mission received £10 a year from the editors of the paper in payment for advertising the *Sunday* and the Reverend Swinstead was delighted to be able to make money for the mission so easily.

He was an economical man. His budget for St Andrew's Mission in 1894 showed that the cost of maintaining the moving parish was £260 8s 7d. His salary, paid by the St Andrew's Society, was £130. The assistant he took with him earned £25 13s 0d and the hire of horses cost another £30. Provisions and household necessities ran to £27 16s 0d and along with the other expenses of insurance, tolls and fees for admission to the fairgrounds, and school equipment for teaching the children, the whole was cheaper than a stationary parish would have been for the same number of people, which was estimated to be about £1000, although it was hard to be exact about the figures in the

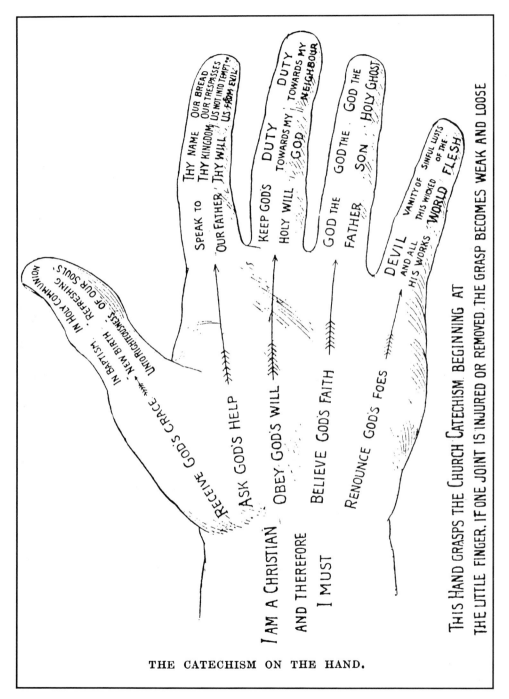

THE CATECHISM ON THE HAND.

The Reverend Swinstead tried to find ways to teach his religion to the gypsies that would make it easy for them to understand.

The interior of the Reverend Swinstead's van resembled as nearly as possible the study of a typical Victorian vicarage, with its books, harmonium and tracts on the wall.

circumstances. The Reverend Swinstead was extremely sympathetic to the gypsies and enjoyed their company. He understood that they had different ways of seeing life, and that strange habits did not necessarily carry the same meaning for the gypsy as that inferred by outsiders. Swinstead never locked his van, because he believed implicitly in the honesty of the travellers, and he dismissed the theory that they were sluttish and dirty. He told a story of a baptism he held, at which a little girl was presented in spotless clothes but with filthy hands. When he asked the reason, the parents explained that they kept the hands unwashed so that they could more easily read the birth lines of their child. In an attempt to teach the gypsies the parables and the Christian message in language that they understood, he made a diagram of the articles of catechism on the outline of an outspread hand, marking the knuckles and fingers with different aspects of the connected parts of the faith. This proved immensely popular and the vicar overheard one traveller say to another as they passed the caravan bookstand where a copy of his catechism was displayed, 'Oh look! here's fortune-tellin' by Mr Swizzleum.'

Although he was very fond of his flock and deeply committed to the care of them, the Reverend Swinstead was never one of the people, and he did not attempt to live like a gypsy in his van.

He was a gentleman, and he shared many of the expectations and opinions of men such as Dr Gordon Stables and Sir Samuel Baker. He was kinder, and more liberal in his thinking, but he still belonged to a world of privilege in which servants were a normal part of the pattern of existence. He published in his book the rules that he gave to his assistants as their terms of employment.

Assistants' Timetable

7.30.	Take down beds, pack away blankets, etc., fold in quilt. Lay breakfast.
8.	Breakfast.
8.30.	Prayers.
8.45-9.30.	Clean up van, breakfast things, four wicks and five candles. Scrub out the van twice a week, and whenever necessary.
9.30-10.30.	Clean the paint inside and out once a week, and whenever necessary. Keep everything well dusted; clean the stove once a week; keep the filter full.
10.30.	Prepare for dinner, and do shopping.
11.30.	Cook dinner.
1.	Dinner.

1.30-4.30.   Finish anything left undone in the morning.
    4.30.   Tea.
    8.30.   Supper.
    10.   Prayers.
   10.30.   Lights out.

Duties at Odd Times

Sell books and give away tracts.
Arrange books in locker below.
Take dogs for a swim.
Brush clothes, mend linen, wash towels, tea-cloths, dusters, etc.
Keep elastic straps fresh on the walls.
Keep books under their right prices on the shelves.

General Rules

Wear straw mission-hat whenever on a message or doing the mission-
work, but not while at work on the van.
Clean plates, dishes, etc., at the basin under the filter.
Stand off the van when you polish boots and shoes (*the springs of the van were
so responsive to any shaking that it was 'sea on land' not to keep this rule*).
Everything is to go back to its place at once, nothing being put under
cushions or mattresses.
Every breakage must be mended at the first stopping-place.
Take washing to laundry immediately on arrival (*the 'laundry' is not always a
modest enough term for the cottage or back garden, where one's more intimate
garments are scrubbed thin, and of course, rent previously to their being mercilessly
spread to dry on the nearest gooseberry-bush or thickset hedge. How I have groaned
to witness it! But it is greater pain to find one's fingers and toes emerging from
these amateur holes, instead of through those specially designed for that purpose*).
Visitors are always to be asked to sign the book.
Ask, if you do not understand.
When seeking horses, take my card with you.

Private to the Use of Rev. J.H.S.

Coloured blankets.
Eiderdown quilt (the special gift of one who likes 'to think of you being
warm').
Large sponge.
Middle locker under berth.
Lower berth.
Writing-table – 'library and study'.

They show an arrogance that came from his class rather than his own nature, but they were severe enough to rankle some of his employees (the italicized comments, incidentally, are the Reverend's own). He had seven assistants in all on his caravan journeys, four of whom left when they found they could not put up with the rigours of the road. Like Dr Gordon Stables' valet, the vicar's assistant was required to be a total abstainer from alcohol and to stick rigorously, on pain of dismissal, to a busy and restrictive schedule. The difference between the doctor's and the clergyman's servant was not in his duties but in his master. The Reverend Swinstead would be up and about and busy for as many hours as his man, and even if he were not prepared to tolerate insubordination he showed a degree of interest in his servant.

While the St Andrew's Mission attempted to reach out to the gypsies from the conventional world, some gypsies were themselves converted and became preachers to their own kind. Gypsy Smith, who was born in a tent in 1860, became an evangelist at seventeen and worked for the Salvation Army until he was dismissed over a misunderstanding about the acceptance of a gold watch from his grateful congregation. He continued as a preacher, and at one time stayed with the family of Silvester Boswell. Boswell wrote in his autobiography about his parents, who became evangelists and were hired by the Free Trade Hall of Manchester to run a gypsy mission. Most of their pay came from the collection, but they also received a small cheque each month and were initially presented with a magnificent wagon, with mahogany panels and three doors which were placed so that it was possible to walk straight in at the front and out at the back. There were double shafts, which were needed for the two horses required to pull the great weight of over three tons. Both Silvester Boswell's father and his mother preached, and his sister Laura played the harmonium, which was kept inside the van and was a vital part of the equipment of this and most other successful mission outfits.

Boswell's parents were converted originally by John Wesley Baker, a man known as a gypsy evangelist, but who was not in fact born a traveller. His caravan and tent were the very ones that the Boswells eventually ended up with, courtesy of the Free Trade Hall, who hired them after they lost faith in John Wesley Baker. Until their conversion, the Boswells lived in Blackpool, where they made a living largely out of palmistry, canework, and whatever came along in the way of horse-trading. They travelled in the summer months and, like most gypsies, stayed in town in the winter, living in their van in a side road or a yard. On 14 February each year, they started to get ready for the road by washing the wagon and polishing the harness. This pattern of life changed forever when they had been converted. They forsook Blackpool and began to travel in earnest. When they joined the Lord, they signed the pledge and they took their vows seriously. They saw Blackpool as a town of wicked

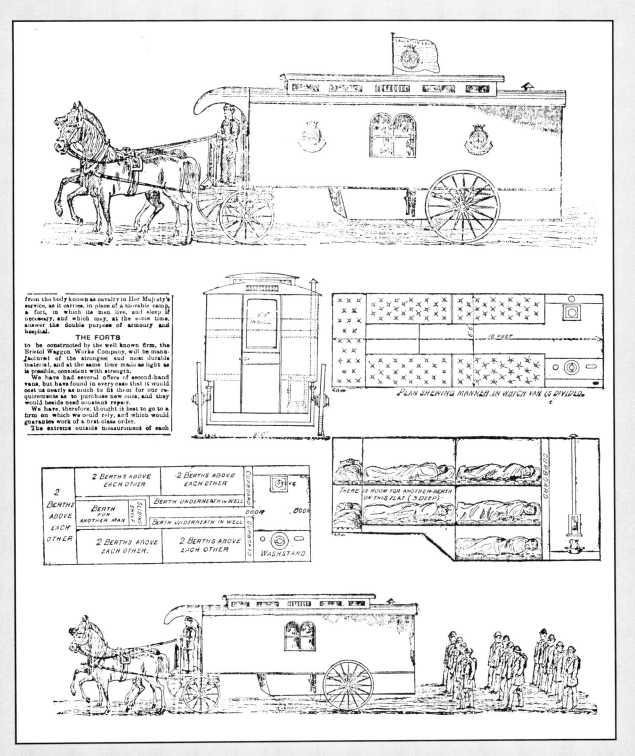

These diagrams were published by the Salvation Army in its magazine War Cry *to launch the campaign for funds for the caravan 'forts'. There was never any shortage of volunteers to travel in them round the country.*

amusements and multiple temptations, so they turned their backs on it for good. Until 1912 they continued to run the mission, and may well have met up with the Salvation Army forts and the Reverend Swinstead at the fairs. If they looked picturesque enough, then they might also have met another group of caravanners of the period, the artists, who took on the bohemian lifestyle of the gypsies and who delighted in painting gypsy portraits.

CHAPTER 6

TRAVELLING ARTISTS

Gypsies were very much the vogue for painters at the turn of the century. The sitters gained esteem from the eminence of the men who sketched them and were proud to have been chosen. It is in general frowned on by gypsies to have a likeness taken, on the principal that it weakens the sitter when his face is caught by the picture, but there seem to have been many gypsies who were happy enough to allow their portraits to be painted. When Sir Alfred Munnings, who was later to be elected President of the Royal Academy, was introduced to a gypsy family called Gray at the Bungay (Essex) races, he was told that the mother, Kiomi, had modelled for Frederick Sandys already, and he was suitably impressed. He was thrilled by the colours and dazzle of their elaborately decorated green and gold caravan, and by the black silk, feathered hats and big gold earrings that the women wore. But he was equally attracted to the bright silk colours of the jockeys, and the thousands of oranges displayed for sale on stalls around the race course, which blazed in the sunlight. The gypsies presented a pleasing picture for him, and he liked them for it, but took no deeper interest in their way of life.

He later bought himself a caravan, a 'proper' one, as he described it, with a stove-pipe sticking out through the roof, and this he took on a summer painting trip to the Ringland Hills in Norfolk. A groom called Bob travelled with him, and he also brought a small fellow with the unlikely name of Fountain Page, who was known as Shrimp. He was nominally in charge of the horses, but his main function for Sir Alfred was as a model. The caravan stayed on the hill all summer, but only Bob and Shrimp lived in it. Sir Alfred was no bohemian. He spent his nights at the nearby Falcoln Inn, and also ate his meals there. He was really only interested in the caravan as a charming backdrop for his real passion, which he reserved for horses. He loved them to look at and to ride. He liked going to the races to see them, and he was a very keen huntsman all his life. Horses were what he enjoyed painting, too, and his pictures during the summer on the hills were all of Shrimp galloping along hell for leather over the grass, full of the joy of motion. Shrimp drank a lot, he chased girls, and at one time Munnings even had to pay a fine for him when the police arrived with the intention of arresting him to face trial on drunk and disorderly charges. Despite the drawbacks, Munnings developed a real affection for his model. He needed to keep him there until the pictures were completed and he was ready to tolerate almost any nuisance that occurred. When one of the horses, an old white Welsh mare, broke her fetlock in a hole on a wooden bridge during the summer and had to be shot, Shrimp cried, and Sir Alfred was moved to see that he did so. He himself had great compassion for his horses. When the height of the summer brought out the flies, he put his mare into the stables at the Falcoln Inn and travelled to his outdoor studio each day by bicycle. He did so because the mare had a docked tail and would have been unable to swish off the flies that plagued her. When he got back each evening to the inn, he went to fetch her from the stable and rode her through the evening in the meadows while the air was cool, so that she got some exercise.

At the end of the summer, when he was preparing to leave, Sir Alfred decided to give the blue caravan to Shrimp, along with the dun horse and its harness. He felt very pleased with his pictures and wanted Shrimp somehow to share in his pleasure. Since he knew that Shrimp had never owned anything in his life, he thought that the pride he gained from becoming the proprietor of a van and horse might cure him of his feckless ways and give him a start in the world. Duly grateful, Shrimp departed, while Sir Alfred remained at the Falcoln for another night. The next morning an innkeeper from a nearby village arrived, asking if he would like to buy back his caravan and horse. When Sir Alfred showed some surprise and questioned him further, the innkeeper explained that Shrimp had become very drunk indeed the night before in his pub, and had sold the lot for next to nothing.

Munnings did not take the van back. He would have had no use for it. He was eventually lured into actually travelling in a caravan, but in different circumstances. A wealthy woman friend, who had studied art at Augustus John's school of art in Chelsea, went by van each September from her country house in Hampshire to the hop fields, to sketch the gypsy hop-pickers who gathered there. She rambled in luxury, in a magnificently carved *vardo* driven by two sleek and well kept horses, and with an able attendant to deal with all the anxieties of the road. At her invitation Sir Alfred took to accompanying her each year on the trip to Binsted, but the outing was far from bohemian and simply offered a pleasant diversion in the country in good company, with some interesting models into the bargain.

This light-hearted Edwardian approach towards caravan life was in direct contrast to the way that the artist Augustus John reacted to the call of the road. He loved gypsies and everything to do with them, and he tried to find out as much as he could about their thinking, their songs and their motivation, in order to become a *rai*, or non-blood brother, to a people who seemed to possess the secret of an antidote to an ugly, industrialized world.

Augustus John was born in Wales in 1877, and he found the life there with his stiff, shy father quite suffocating. His mother died when he was small and he was brought up by two aunts, both of whom held rank in the Salvation Army. He escaped to London and the Slade School of Art. There he performed brilliantly, particularly after a diving accident in which he seriously injured his skull. Myths spread about the possible effect that a bang on the head could have on creating a genius and changing a personality; it was certainly true that his character altered after the accident. He grew a beard, wore earrings and an old smoking cap, and acted in an increasingly flamboyant manner. In *Augustus John: A Biography* the author Michael Holroyd describes how John, at about this time, was followed in the street by a group of children who were attracted by his great height and his scruffy appearance. They began shouting: 'Get yer 'air cut, mister,' at which Augustus John halted, turned on them and growled: 'Get your throats cut.'

At the Slade he met and fell in love with a fellow student, Ida Nettleship. They married and went together to Liverpool, where John took up a post as instructor at an art school affiliated to University College. In 1901 he met the university librarian John Sampson, who was a passionate student of gypsy lore. He had trained himself in Romany and in Shelta, the language of the tinkers, and he had gathered information from many of the gypsies that he knew for the Gypsy Lore Society and its journal. Even when the journal was in abeyance he continued to build his knowledge on the subject, and by the time that John met him he was a formidable expert on the subject. He took the young artist to Cabbage Hall, a strip of wasteland outside town where many gypsies stayed during the winter. The attraction that these people held for Augustus John was instant and overwhelming. He did not fully understand what drew him so powerfully, again and again, to Cabbage Hall, but he found that he was endlessly fascinated by the tales and customs in the camp. He loved stories like the one about the beautiful gypsy, Esmeralda Groome (née Boswell), who was forced to marry a rich middle-class man she did not love then ran off with Francis Hindes Groome, a writer, to roam Europe while he wrote books with such titles as *In Gypsy Tents*. When they finally returned to Scotland and married in Edinburgh, she promptly deserted him for the lure of the open road, despite his frantic efforts to keep her. Her wildness, her lack of convention and her elusiveness all removed her from the prim world of Edwardian England, where wives worried about their honour and still belonged as chattels to their husbands. In her waywardness, Esmeralda showed all the qualities that John desired in a woman.

He hated convention. His genuine lack of concern about the world's opinion of his conduct (which was one of shocked fascination) did not inhibit his growing success as an artist. He managed to obtain portrait commissions while he lived with both his wife Ida and his mistress Dorelia, to whom he had written love letters in Romany (despite the fact that she was by birth Dorothy McNeill of Camberwell and needed an annotated list of words at the end of the letters so that she could understand them). Dorelia's first child, Pyramus, was born in a caravan that John had purchased from a fellow art student who used it himself for his honeymoon. The baby spent his first summer in the middle of Dartmoor with his family, while Ida nursed Dorelia back to health after the confinement.

Augustus John fathered son after son by his women, between ramblings that took him all round Europe in search of gypsies. In France, where the family often accompanied him, he took his summer guest, the writer Wyndham Lewis, along to the camps. In Spain he became fascinated by flamenco music, songs and dancing. He learned to play flamenco from a gypsy guitarist, Fabian de Castro, and collected details of songs to send back to his friends in Liverpool where the Gypsy Lore Society's journal had been revived by Roger Andrew Scott Macfie, who had given up a job as head of a firm of sugar-refiners to devote himself to the venture. In Italy, where he attended a huge feast of all the tribes at Milan, John wrote to Scott Macfie about the occasion and tried to convey his feeling about the music in words such as 'natural', 'religious' and 'orgiastic'. He also saw W.B. Yeats, who was obsessed by the tinkers, and Lady Gregory, who collected information about myths and dialects, when he went to Ireland, a country with a very high proportion of travellers.

Ida died in childbirth in France, and Augustus John and Dorelia returned to England to live. They muddled along together, with an increasing clutch of children. Their chaotic lifestyle was hard work for Dorelia, but she was an extraordinarily tranquil woman, with a mysterious stillness that shows in John's paintings of her. She seemed able to deal with infidelity, abandonment, bad temper and constant movement with serenity. She believed in Augustus John's great ability as a painter and felt that his genius gave him the right to behave as he chose.

In the summer of 1910, John decided it was time for the family to go on the road again. He collected together the van that Pyramus was born in, now repainted sky blue, added a canary-yellow one and a light cart, two tents and a team of six old omnibus horses and set off to meet Dorelia, her sister Edie, six children and a groom. They all assembled at Effingham, where John was proud to see that the camp was like that of the mumpers, or tinkers – only more untidy. They moved on to Derby to protest, unsuccessfully, about the exclusion of gypsies from the race course on Derby Day, then went via Harpenden to Cambridge, where they camped in a field by a river at Grantchester. John had a commission to paint Miss Jane Harrison, the classical anthropologist, at Newnham College.

The caravan caused a great deal of interest in Cambridge. Some people were glad to see the family and clearly welcomed them. The poet Rupert Brooke took the family on the river. Gilbert Murray chatted to Augustus John while he painted, and Miss Harrison herself was friendly, and liked her portrait. Others were less charitable and treated them more as a sideshow than anything else. Maynard Keynes spread rumours that there were two wives and ten naked children in the camp, and others said that well-known academic families of Cambridge, like the Raverats and the Verralls, made special journeys to the fields to catch a glimpse of the party. They saw Dorelia making Turkish trousers and the children sitting around the fire gnawing on

Gypsy scenes like this one, showing decorated hats on dark-skinned women and pointed chimneys on gaily painted vans, greatly appealed to painters at the turn of the century.

Augustus John was introduced to the gypsies by John Sampson, the 'gypsy expert', whilst he was teaching art in Liverpool.

bones for their supper before falling asleep on straw that had been strewn about. Word spread that John had been involved in a drunken brawl in the street, and in fact he did get a black eye after a fight with the groom he had hired, Arthur, who was not an ideal employee. The extraordinary Lady Ottoline Morrell, who was obsessed by the artistic figures of her day and greatly admired John, whom she pursued round London for some time, arrived to stay in the caravan the day after the fight. She found everyone morose, unwelcoming and unprepared to make her a decent dinner. She left the next day; Augustus John also absconded, to Liverpool, by train, leaving Dorelia to cope with camp life in a damp field on her own, while he painted a portrait of his old friend Chaloner Dowdall, the retiring Lord Mayor of Liverpool.[4]

By the end of the summer two of the horses had died, and all the boys had caught whooping cough. Even for the John family, who were eager to live as gypsies and ready to accept different standards of hygiene and habit, life proved extremely fraught. They were not, and never could be, gypsies. The culture that intrigued them and the Gypsy Lore Society was not their own; indeed, a lot of its attraction lay in that very fact. More and more people felt, like them, that modern life was going horribly wrong, and searched for alternative lifestyles that would offer an escape from the age of mammon.

CHAPTER 7

THE GOOD LIFE

When Matthew Arnold wrote, in 'The Scholar Gypsy', this strange disease of modern life, with its sick hurry, its divided aims,' his words struck a deep chord in many people who were also sickened by the crude and materialistic values of late nineteenth-century society, and repelled by families who crammed into the semi-detached villas surrounded by their booty. Lives of dullness, respectability, thrift and ceaseless industry had given them the money to stuff dark parlours with antimacassars, pianos, velveteen drapes and potted plants. The daily paper, one of the new plebian gossip sheets, arrived full of stories about the misfortunes of the fallen to satisfy the morbid curiosity of a smug and ostensibly virtuous public. More thoughtful papers, like the *Saturday Review*, published articles expressing the fear that while the masses had found physical improvement in their conditions, their moral health had declined. The demonstratins held after the Peace Day at the end of the South African War in 1902, with mobs baying like wild animals in the street, seemed to offer proof of a universal unease about moral decay.

Nationalism grew strong. All foreigners were regarded with suspicion, or accused, on sight, of terrorist intentins. Anarchists were blamed for bank robberies, staged to get money to finance mayhem and revolution. When they were not searching for scapegoats to blame for the degeneration of the species, people clung to their roots, to the pure simplicity of their early ancestors. Folk tales were especially popular, and in countries such as America, where they had no folk tales of their own except those of the Red Indians, they borrowed those imported with the immigrants. Stories like 'Rip Van Winkle' and 'Hiawatha' came to be as American as apple pie. The American Indian, hounded almost to extinction during the previous hundred years, was given the new image of 'nature's gentleman' and idealized by Fenimore Cooper in his books. Clubs and societies were formed to teach children the skills of the Indian scouts. A generation before, the pioneers had still known how to survive on the prairie by their own wits, but now that towns and the railway had brought easy access to goods and services, the young Americans quickly forgot how to use a knife in the pursuit and preparation of food, or to make a

*The old-established firms of carriage-builders made heavy, beautifully crafted caravans. The new
breed of caravanner wanted a much lighter vehicle.*

shelter in the open. At other times in history, no one would have felt it necessary to remember, but worried parents, afraid that their boys would become weak and dissolute members of an effete society, made sure that they went off to camps to learn the lessons of simple manly virtue as displayed by the Indian brave.

In Britain, Bade-Powell heard about the camps in which boys tracked, became Masters of Woodcraft and won badges after tests of skill, and he decided to start a movement of his own for English boys. He ran an experimental camp in 1907 on Brownsea Island, where boys from different classes mixed together. They heard stories about hoeroes of the past, then split into groups, or packs, with names like 'Curlews', 'Ravens', 'Wolves' and 'Bulls'. They competed at swimming and trials of skill and strength, learned first aid, imitated animal and bird noises and, above all, conducted these activities in an atmosphere of fair play. Woken in the morning by a blast from the koodoo horn Baden-Powell had brought back from Matabeleland, they tumbled out into the fresh air into days full of fun and activity. Baden-Powell had hoped to reach the boys in the sulms with his Boy Scout movement, but sadly it was the middle classes who mainly responded to the programme he offered to their sons. These children, the first fruit of the twentieth century, who dreamed about motor cars and yachts and all the trappings of the new industrial barons, were happy enough to join in with Baden-Powell's ideas. Solemnly they learned tribal incantatins and practised lighting a camp fire by rubbing two sticks together, following trails and constructing shelters.

While the children played at being Indians, some of their elders tried to create private worlds of their own, away from the harsh realities of modern life. They attempted to form utopian societies and co-operative movements where values corresponded more closely to a way of life that they could admire. They consciously changed not only the rules they lived by, but their actual physical environment. William Morris and his Arts and Crafts movement sought to pare down clutter to the absolute essentials – in furniture, in dress and even in social habits. They believed that an ideal future could be found by turning the best of the past into the reality of the present. All the utopians were essentially socialist. Rank was abolished (although there were often leaders who ruled by virtue of moral strength); people worked because of the joy to be found in labour, particularly at jobs in the open air which required physical action. Fresh air and fit bodies wee an integral part of healthy lives. Plain food, loose clothing and daily exercise would purge the mind of the trivia of existence and leave it purified, open to the voice of nature. 'Our life is frittered away by detail . . . simplify, simplify,' Henry Thoreau advised. This philosophy bred a new cult, which was mocked and ridiculed unmercifully by conventional society, of men and women who followed the Simple Life.

The most extreme examples of Simple Lifers were men like Edward Carpenter, a man born into easy circumstances in 1884 and educated at Cambridge, where he became first a fellow of his college, then a curate. Having read Walt Whitman's *Leaves of Grass* at the same time as he suffered a sort of nervous breakdown, he was deeply affected by its philosophy of returning to nature, and decided to throw up his career and move to a labourer's cottage in Sheffield. Here he worked in the fields and as a mechanic. He also started to make sandals, to a design that he had seen in India when he travelled there to sit at the feet of a guru. These proved to be very popular amongst other Simple Lifers and his work was in much demand. After the day's work, Edward Carpenter wrote poetry, or lectured on his theories at workmen's institutes, adult education classes and similar venues. He told his listeners that health was a positive 'wholeness' rather than an absence of disease. A man should be at one with himself, with his soul reigning at the centre of a body well tuned to keep all passions and desires in balance. He spoke in favour of pacifism, sex reform, vegetarianism, penal reform, emancipation of women and smoke abatement, and gathered a large number of disciples to his causes. He lived his final days in a cottage, cultivating his garden and sharing his home with a labourer called George Merrill, who had been born in the Sheffield slums, and who was the object of Carpenter's unswerving affection all his adult life. By this time he had fallen out with mainstream socialists of his generation, men like Bernard Shaw, who wanted to adopt a more political attitude. Living in isolation, he saw the sandals he made as statements of liberation – not political, but life-giving. They freed the foot, he sincerely believed, by releasing it from the boot, symbol of the husk that mankind must shrug off like a snake shedding its skin in order to reach the next stage of development. Carpenter did not believe in the evolution of man, or in Darwin's monkeys, but thought that the human species slowly unfurled like a leaf, going through necessary convulsions on the way, some ugly, some beautiful, until it blossomed into full maturity.

Not everyone would wish to go so far as Edward Carpenter on his journey away from normal life, but there were plenty of people who espoused some, if not all, of the theories of Simple Life. One of these was Bertram Smith, who followed Thoreau's advice about simplifying, and applied it to the caravan. He designed his own, having ruthlessly done away with all thought of gypsy-like ornamentation. His first priority was mobility, so he discarded any aspect of the van that could not be considered strictly functional. His first caravan was called 'Triumvir', and it was light enough to move at ten miles an hour, pulled by one horse at a steady trot. It weighed only a ton unloaded, even though it was 18 feet long and had space for three good-sized rooms. The walls were whitewood panels, the roof constructed of Willesden canvas, the springs and carriage wheels as light as could be manufactured, and he

Advertisers, quick to realize how lucrative the caravan market was, adapted their products to suit the needs of gentlemen gypsies. The disposal of waste, and sanitary arrangements in particular, posed problems for all travellers.

described the result, in his book *The Whole Art of Caravanning*, as 'light as a feather, dainty as a yacht, and spacious withal', looking from the outside like a 'piece of drawing-room furniture'. He divided people into three sorts, 'those who can caravan, those who can't and a small group of true nomads and vagabonds, who must'. He personally found the accumulation of earthly belongings to be the one great bar to freedom of action, and felt a kindred spirit with the third category.

He was quite ready to offer advice to the amateur, however: useful information, such as warning people of the dangers of collapsible beds; not to choose too high a structure for their van because it could easily be blown over in a strong wind; not to park on wet grass with rubber tyres in case they perished; and to remember that in order to carry a piano, you certainly would need to take another horse. He told his readers, when they were loading up for the trip, to think of Jerome K. Jerome's *Three Men in a Boat*. Pack 'enough to eat, and enough to smoke, and a little more than enough to drink. For thirst is a dangerous thing.'

He adored cooking, and prided himself on being able to produce a five-course dinner for four from an oil-stove with two burners and an oven. He outlined the duties that should be shared by the travellers. The Coachman had special care of the horses and held supreme command, and the whip, whilst on the road. He was required to walk beside the horse most of the time, whistling, ready to hop on the platform, at the front of the caravan from time to time to put on or take off the brake. No self-respecting coachman rode in the van, except when it was travelling downhill. If he stayed aboard at any other time, he could never again look his horse straight in the eye. The Ambassador was expected to argue the party out of trouble, and to wheedle them on to good camping grounds. The Forager went off by bike in search of fresh eggs and milk, while the Housemaid dried hankies on the glass of the window and did the washing-up. All these jobs passed round in rotation, but the one unchangeable office was that held by the Cook. He cleaned his own stove and created memorable dishes on it for his hungry friends. Supper was not a mere meal, to fill the undoubtedly empty belly at the end of a long day's march, but a ceremony to be treated with the greatest respect. Square eggs, van-pot and half-volley savoury needed to be given their time to mature if they were to provide the fullest enjoyment. Bertram Smith wrote a poem, with which he was very pleased, about the joys of cooking on a caravan trip.

I love the gentle office of the cook,
The cheerful stove, the placid twilight hour,
When, with the tender fragrance of a flower,
And all the bubbling voices of the brook,

The coy potato, or the onion browns,
The tender steak takes on a nobler hue,
I ponder mid the falling of the dew,
And watch the lapwings circling o'er the downs.

Like portals at the pathway of the moon,
Two trees stand forth, in pencilled silhouette,
Against the steel-grey sky, as black as jet –
The steak is ready. Ah! too soon! too soon![5]

Since the caravan was built so that the front panels were movable, it was possible, after the meal was over and cleared away, to sit on deckchairs up on the platform with the panels open, raised up above the hedges where the views were so much better, and watch the sun set at the end of a lovely day.

Bertram Smith was not such a caravan fanatic that he could not admit that some people found the daily chores a nuisance. They would prefer to take a valet along, especially if they were going to spend their days fishing, or golfing, or sketching. Then, although the caravan was the centre to which they always returned, they were free to diverge by day and collect for the long summer evenings when they wished. But he felt that for the complete caravanner, part of the game was the work required to keep the van clean and the horses fit. He was a friendly and hospitable man, quite ready to travel with companions and totally insistent that a dog should always be on hand, but he was probably happiest on his own. He took no map to guide him on the way, he made no arrangements for the receipt of letters, he stopped his watch before setting off, threw away his diary, and even made detours round market towns that had clocks on their church towers, in case he accidentally noticed the time. The true accolade of a successful traveller was if he actually forgot what day of the week and month it was. He naturally avoided newspapers at all costs. In this way, he explained, a man 'without crossing the Andes or the upper waters of the Nile can create a new world for himself and explore it'.

Naturally, Smith did not dress smartly while he was on one of his trips, and was often mistaken for something other than a touring gentleman. His van was once thought to be a prison van, and a woman in the crowd that gathered in one village exclaimed that it was scandalous that prisoners should be allowed to be so comfortable at ratepayers' expense. Another time, in Prestatyn in North Wales, he was followed by a great mass of people all the way through the town until he reached the railway station, where he was arrested by a policeman and marched in handcuffs into the ladies' waiting-room. The townsfolk, it seems, were convinced he was an escaped lunatic.

Despite some eccentric ways, he was quite sensible about his ideas for the caravan, and by the early 1900s he had built several, enough to constitute a small fleet; all were plain boxes without stoves or domed roofs, which he hired out in the summer months at reasonable prices. This was the last straw for John Sampson, the friend of Augustus John and gypsy expert. He had been horrified to see the traditional gypsy wagon pared down to a travesty of functionalism. He called this style of caravan a blot on the landscape and added, in his diatribe against Bertram Smith, 'there is still hope for him if he could be persuaded to learn Romani, be less of an epicure, take his bath in the open, burn his detestable removing van, and replace it with a decent Gypsy vardo.'

Baths were a hotly contested issue at the time. Bertram Smith approved of them, and took his in the main saloon of the van, which had been designed so that all the chairs and tables hinged on to the wall and could be put out of the way when he wished to erect his india-rubber bath. In the front of his book, *The Whole Art of Caravanning*, appears an advertisement for Dr Gustav Jaeger's Sanitary Woollen System, a form of clothing that was favoured by the boys in Dr Gordon Stables' novel *Cruise of the Rover Caravan*. The German doctor who invented this 'system' had very strong views about baths. He thought, like others at the time, that baths were enervating, and he advised against the need for them, except at infrequent intervals, and then only if the bather came out of the bath immediately and donned his Sanitary Woollen System outfit without drying himself first, or, even better, soaked the clothes so that they were wringing wet when he put them on. This would have been pretty exhausting because wet clothes are difficult to wriggle into at the best of times, as anyone who has tried to put back on a wet bathing suit at the beach will know; but if the outfit includes a close-cut buttoned woollen shirt, tight-fitting trousers with webbed bottoms to ensure that air cannot seep in from below, socks with individual compartments for each toe, and shoes with woollen uppers, then the task becomes almost impossible.

Dr Jaeger insisted that his followers wear this outfit at all times, winter and summer, in order to allow the noxious essences to escape the body. The woollen casing to the body kept the skin uniformly warm, offered a free outlet for the 'cutaneous evaporation', gently titillated the skin to encourage the blood supply, and helped with the shedding of the outer cuticle. Since the noxious excretions were allowed to escape, the body remained healthy and free of all the horrors that these fumes produced to the system. Gloom, depression, want of courage and lack of appetite could be avoided. Disease was rebuffed, he averred, for just as fleas prefer the taste of certain flesh, so the epidemic illnesses love to feast on the noxious-smelling bodies of the uninitiated. In the same way that defeated armies were more prone to disease than their jubilant conquerors, the melancholy wearer of cotton or linen next to the skin was more likely to draw cholera and typhoid into his person than Dr Jaeger's happy converts. The Sanitary Woollen System could also help people to lose weight, particularly when worn in the summer months. It could be noticed, at first, when a person embarked on the System, and walked through the midday sun in tightly buttoned woollens, that he smelled very strongly and unpleasantly, but this passed once the noxious elements had evaporated and the salutary essences reigned supreme in his body. The clothing did not even need cleaning very often. It could be hung on a line in the garden and whacked like a carpet.

For safety's sake, the System applied as rigorously at night as by day. In a room with all the windows thrown open, the strict adherent, from the days of the cradle onwards, would lie tossing on woollen sheets laid over a mattress stuffed with wool, and, if he were bald, in a woollen nightcap. Dr Jaeger quoted the old German proverb that a healthy, comfortable man was 'sitting in the wool' as proof of the efficacy of his System, and all round Europe men and women were convinced that he was right. They marched up mountains, purple in the face but pure in their emanations; swam in rivers buttoned up to the neck in soggy self-righteousness; and wrapped themselves up against the summer breezes wafting in through the caravan windows in woollen sheets that no one had washed for months. Strangely, Dr Jaeger was keen on meat.

His poor family, who were used as guinea-pigs for all his ideas, were allowed to eat well and were never heard to report that their essences were sullied by the consumption of steak. The Doctor, who constantly mentioned the troubles that he had with his widening waistline, may well have been a big eater. If he found it impossible to give up his favourite dishes, he may have considered it prudent to pronounce that meat was healthy for all comers in case he was ever cornered in a restaurant by one of his disciples just as he tucked into his veal and onions.

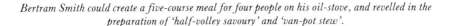

Bertram Smith could create a five-course meal for four people on his oil-stove, and revelled in the preparation of 'half-volley savoury' and 'van-pot stew'.

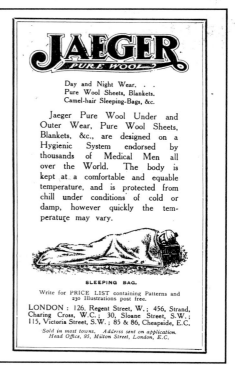
The Contour Road Books *showed where the steep hills were, which helped travellers to avoid getting stuck half-way up and then ignominiously sliding down to the bottom. The Jaeger Sanitary Woollen System, on the other hand, was very popular with health-conscious caravanners.*

His advice would have found little favour with another caravanner of the period, a man called Bertram Hutchings; he would later have an important part to play in the history of the caravan, but was at that time following the Simple Life and running a food reformist shop with his wife in Winchester.

The people who followed the teachings and lived plain lives, with even plainer clothes and food, infuriated the more political rebels of their generation. This was the first time socialism had begun to reach any kind of audience in Britain, and when the people started to exercise some degree of influence on the affairs of government. For those involved it was a mighty and righteous cause and they could not understand why others would choose to stand back and lead lives outside the political arena. The Trade Union movement slowly gained momentum, the Fabian Society flourished, and the Labour Party laid the ground for the momentous election of 1906 when it managed to obtain over forty seats in Parliament. Women pressed for rights of property and for the vote, at first with seemly gentility, then – after the arrival in their movement in 1903 of the Pankhurst family, mother and daughters –

with sudden fury. All round the country, after the setting up of parish councils in 1894, local elections depended on the votes of the ordinary working men, who could put up their own Radical candidate if they wished to stand against the Conservative. Marxists, anarchists and socialists roamed about preaching the gospel of social revolution. Some of them travelled in caravans, which they kept stuffed with tracts, and from the platforms of which they harangued the crowds. At first they received short shrift in the villages, where they were laughed off the greens and pelted with rotten eggs. An almost feudal system still controlled life for the poor outside the cities, and at first no one dared to have opinions that contradicted the views prevailing in the big house.

Richard Whiteing used the first parish elections as the setting for his novel *The Yellow Van*, a book which ably illustrates the mood of the time. The story is set in a mythical village called Slocum Parva, which stands in the curtilage of the country house of Slocum, seat of the handsome Lord Allonby. The yellow van of the title is owned by a Radical politician and his family who arrive at the village at the time of the elections to speak about 'the restoration of the land to the people, and of the people to the land'. The Radical has trouble finding anywhere to leave his caravan, or to hold a meeting, but is patient in the face of his difficulties. He is mild and well educated, and he quietly endures the jeering he receives when he finally does speak to the crowds of Slocum Parva. One listener, a young man who works as a ploughboy for Lord Allonby, is fired by enthusiasm for what he hears and shouts out his approval in public. The consequences for him are dire. While the apathetic Lord and his pretty American wife are away in London, the wicked overseer of the estate dismisses George, who has recently married the vivacious beauty of the village. They are forced to leave and go to London in search of work, where they struggle and suffer in the slums, drawn down a relentless spiral of poverty and disease until they meet their separate and ghastly fates. Eventually Lord and Lady Allonby, racked with guilt over the treatment their employees have received in their name, trace the couple in time to bring home the wife's body and the grotesquely maimed George.

Although the story is melodramatic in the extreme, the book was not written to discourage Radical action, however dire the consequences inflicted upon the hapless George, but rather to shock the reader into a better understanding of the anomalies of life in Britain and the appalling power still wielded by a fading aristocracy and their cruel land agents. The caravan, bobbing in and out of the narrative, is like a small boat on the sea in a storm, bringing aid to a stricken liner. It carries the quietly spoken socialist on his journey of hope, enabling him to tell the people that the hour of their liberation is at hand and that the mighty will fall.

Although it carried a twentieth-century man, the caravan in *The Yellow Van* was horse-drawn. A motor-driven one would have been far too expensive for a poor political agitator to afford. In the mansions and ostentatious town houses of the rich, the people whom the socialist despised might however have been toying with the idea of investing in something of the sort. From this time onwards, the new inventions for travel all centred on the engine instead of the horse, and the pace at which life was lived in the twentieth century was matched by the speed of the motor car.

CHAPTER 8

FOUR-LEGGED FRIENDS

The law requiring motor cars to be preceded at all times by a man carrying a red flag was abolished in 1896. In the same year, at the beginning of the first London-to-Brighton race, the Earl of Winchelsea ceremoniously ripped up a red flag to symbolize the delight of the motoring community at the law's repeal. By 1900 the car was a necessary trapping of wealth – still a toy, but about to become a part of everyday existence for many people. The first London cabs appeared on the streets in 1903; motor bicycles roared on to the scene in the same year; the Army decided to look into the military possibilities of the combustion engine; and the public began to travel in motor buses in 1907.

Yet it was inconceivable that the horse would lose its dominance as the nation's means of transport. At exactly the time that the motor car was being developed, the builders of horse-drawn caravans found themselves with more customers than ever before. Books written at the time for the use of pleasure-caravan travellers provided advice on horses for hire, favouring different sources but never once questioning the universal availability of supply. L.C.R. Cameron recommended, in the *Book of the Caravan*, that they be obtained from the Railway Company Agents or from local farmers. Lady Arthur Grosvenor assured her readers in her contribution to *The Campers' Handbook*, compiled by T.H. Holding, that by far the best horses were bought directly from the gypsies. A gypsy 'pal', she claimed, could be trusted, because it was used to travelling long distances and, as it had always known camp life, would have no inclination to stray. An outlay of £20 to £30 would be sufficient, she suggested, to obtain a good specimen. Many gypsies would have been delighted to know that she had published a recommended price guide for enthusiasts. It gave the seller a great advantage to know from the outset of the bargaining the amount that the buyer expected to pay. Commercial travelling companies, like those with theatres and marionette shows, often acquired horses through furniture-removers. The rates for all these various methods of hire varied between 3*d* and 9*d* a day for the horse and man. This seems reasonable, considering that the fee at a farm for the grazing of one's own horse would probably have been at a rate of 6*d* a night.

These horses, hired or bought, inspired great affection in their owners. Most of the people who caravanned and recorded their experiences included some anecdotes about their favourite horses. The pioneer of pleasure caravans, Dr W. Gordon Stables, wrote about his first draught-horse, Matilda, who had only worked at pulling the plough before he obtained her to take himself and two of his children in a trial run in the 'Wanderer'. She went well for two miles, except that she neighed all the time, noisily, as if she were laughing at a secret joke; and then she stopped. Having decided that even if this were the longest field she had ever known it *must* by now be the end of the furrow, she kept trying to turn as she would always have done when ploughing, ready for the return furrow, and nothing would persuade her to be coaxed forward again.

Bertram Smith, the Simple Life adherent, reserved his greatest affection for Black Jim, a city-dweller who spent most of his life in Liverpool hauling cotton bales. Black Jim was completely unmoved by the prospect of an approaching runaway traction engine but would lose his nerve completely at the sight of a plough or a passing flock of sheep. He was placid; Bertram Smith recorded that he had 'an occasional trot in him'; and he proved to be the wrong horse to take along on a tour of Wales.

The hills there were difficult for caravans in any case, being so long and steep. When Black Jim was confronted by a particularly grim mountain road while harnessed to Smith's first caravan, 'Triumvir', he decided to make no attempt to mount it; indeed, he 'sat down and wept' in the road. It was only when a team of four horses was gathered that the caravan reached the summit, 'with all the thunder and *éclat* of a cavalry charge'.

Another Simple Life enthusiast and socialist reformer, Dugald Semple, who lived in a converted omnibus for years before building his own caravan, advised readers of his books to be kind to their horses, and to remember that they were man's 'partner in civilization'. Frances Jennings, a semi-paralysed artist who travelled round the countryside, summer and winter, in a converted coster's barrow drawn by a donkey called Eva, often mentioned the donkey in her letters. The references were full of the irritation that one traveller might well feel for another after several weeks in close proximity and uncomfortable surroundings. She told a friend that one day when Eva reached the bottom of a steep path she lay down between the shafts rather than carry on, and acted as if she were dead. The animal had slumped motionless, but Frances Jennings could see her face from where she lay in the cart, and was aware that with one 'wicked, white gleaming eye she laughed at me'. After shouting for some time, she attracted the attention of two men, who ran, 'all arms and legs, as if I was a house on fire', to help drag Eva on to her

The Ford *by Sir Alfred Munnings*
Sir Alfred installed his favourite model, Shrimp, in a caravan in the Ringland Hills for the summer
so that he could paint a series of pictures of him on horseback. He then gave the caravan to Shrimp as
a friendly gesture.

Campfire and Caravan *by Sir Alfred Munnings*
The picture contains all the necessary ingredients for a popular gypsy scene: a lurcher, a fine horse, a
woman by the campfire and a gaily painted vardo.

A Gypsy Encampment *by Pal Bohm*
This shows Spanish gypsies in a rather romanticized setting. English gypsies would probably have been eating rabbit stew rather than water-melon.

Gypsy Life *by Sir Alfred Munnings*
The artist was fascinated by the bright-coloured clothes and feathered hats of the gypsy
women he painted at the races.

All the Fun of the Fair *by Ernest Proctor*
*As the fairgrounds became more and more mechanized and the entertainment grew fast and furious,
some of the early innocent charm of the stalls and merry-go-rounds was lost for ever.*

Toad's Caravan *by Arthur Rackham*
As was the habit of many Victorian and Edwardian gentlemen, Toad (of Wind in the Willows*)*
moves from one fad to another. His love of the travelling life comes to an end when he discovers the
greater lure of the motor car.

Big Top and Caravans *by E. Heskith Hubbard*
Circus performers often lived in very elaborate vans featuring plush upholstery and carved fireplaces.
The famous clowns and animal trainers mixed with rich and titled admirers.

feet once more. She also wrote, 'I mustn't leave my donkey more than three weeks, or it will get too lazy and wicked for anything.'

Frances sometimes found it necessary to use the whip, but she also understood that her 'poor little donkey' needed to indulge a few pleasures. She noted that Eva had a longing to 'taste the fresh, pale green, spring grass which made her walk crooked from side to side of the road'.[6]

Most horses, and donkeys, had set habits, and when the time came to buy or hire one for a caravan tour it was important to make sure that it would not let the party down at a vital moment. In his contribution to *Caravanning and Camping Out*, Captain C. Hunt advised that a horse should always be given a trial run to see if it jibbed at hills or refused to pass cars or railway trains. He suggested that it was always a sound decision to pick a good eater, because it would stay strong and healthy. He was adamant that tails should never be docked, since the horse was then at the mercy of flies, and he pointed out that a young horse was not necessarily what the van traveller would want. Age and suitability were his watchwords. Different tasks demanded different horses, and it was better to have a quiet, strong horse than a mischievous pony that might slip off its rope in the night and wander into the fields. He also tried to educate his reader on the proper ways to feed a horse. He explained that a horse's gastric juices were different from those of man or dog, and that it needed to feed every three hours or so unless it were to suffer agonies from hunger pangs. It was vital to remember, however, that a horse must drink before eating. Men have always watered the horses first, before setting up camp and feeding them, and for excellent reasons: a horse that drinks within an hour after eating risks colic, which will completely incapacitate it until the pain subsides and render it useless in the meantime. Most horses know instinctively that they must not eat before drinking. Captain Hunt related an incident about a horse that had refused to eat at the end of a long day's march. The owners were baffled as to the cause of the horse's loss of appetite. The next day the horse drank bucket after bucket of water drawn from the first stream that the party passed, then ate until he was fit to burst. It was later discovered that the water offered to him the night before, prior to his meal, was slightly brackish. The horse was unable to drink it, and therefore felt certain that he should also refuse food until such time as he found pure water with which to slake his thirst.

People went to great lengths to ensure the comfort and fitness of their horses. Their relative cost was very high, and those who owned thoroughbreds were prepared to spend a lot on them. By 1908, an English thoroughbred racer had changed hands for the staggering amount of 37,500 guineas, and even a young hunter had been sold for as much as 1,250 guineas. Since such amounts represented a fortune for most of the population, it was only a select few who could hope to run horses of their own. They were very much a

After the showmen switched to moving their caravans by steam, the only horses in the shows were the mechanical ones that they kept for the roundabouts.

The early merry-go-rounds were gentle rides, and horses were the most popular mounts with the public.

symbol of wealth and worldly success. The race horse, particularly, attracted rich patrons. Often of doubtful breeding themselves, self-made millionaires were fascinated by the fine, skittish thoroughbreds upon which they lavished their money. After Edward VII's accession to the throne in 1902, he continued to enjoy the same company that he had shared as Prince of Wales. He liked rich, successful men, and he did not care where they came from as long as they were good company, indulged in sport and gave him sound tips on the stock exchange. Although he enjoyed yachting and shooting immensely, his greatest interest was in horses, and it was a popular passion shared with his people. Every class of Briton understood their attraction, from the gypsy to the farmer, to the tradesman, to the artist, to landed gentry. As a nation the British united in wild jubilation when the King's horse, Minoru, won the Derby, and when the King died the women showed their grief at his passing by attending the races in mourning, causing the Ascot of 1910 to become known as Black Ascot.

Race horses ran for high stakes and could be sold at stud for large fees, so they were watched over meticulously; thousand upon thousand was spent on their stabling and training. But even hunters cost a good deal to keep, and were treated with every loving attention. The hunt was an essential part of the social scene of rural England, and it was necessary to keep horses to be a part of society. Many rich businessmen played at being squires at the weekend. They bought up manor houses and came down from the City on Fridays to indulge in parties or to hunt and shoot and fish. These men might know little about horses, and care less, but they would have to maintain a good stable in order to pass muster with the local gentry, who would probably be fairly resentful of their intrusion in any case.

Many local owners worked with their own horses themselves, and loved them dearly. One such man, Captain W.G. Smith, J.P., D.C., who owned several hunters, felt that sea bathing was good for them, and in 1906 he purchased a caravan so that he could spend a considerable time at Mablethorpe and Sutton-on-Sea each year accompanied by his studsman, in order to give his horses plenty of swimming. He never mentioned whether he or his studsman joined them in the water, but it was clear that the object of the exercise was the health of the hunters.

For men like Captain Smith, and Charles Richardson, the author of *The New Book of the Horse*, it was impossible to imagine that the horse would cease to occupy its place of honour in the hearts of all their countrymen. Mr Richardson, who published his book in 1910, noted that mechanical traffic appeared to be on the increase, and that the birth rate among foals was dropping from year to year. He conceded that it was unlikely that the horse-drawn omnibus would survive against the competition of its motor-operated equivalent, but he failed to believe that the days of the horse were numbered. He reminded his readers that gloom merchants had predicted the demise of horse-drawn transport seventy years previously at the start of the railway age, and they had been confounded. He pointed out that the steam plough had been in use for nearly two generations, but never yet seriously rivalled the horse-drawn plough. He had seen a motor plough in operation some years earlier, near Biggleswade, and it had appeared to work well, but nothing more had come of such machines since then. He knew that the equine military requirement numbered 174,000, of which 59,000 were cavalry horses, and he could think of nothing that could usurp their place on the battlefield. He considered it possible that the towns were suited to the combustion engine, but the countryside would never change. What small tradesman could possibly afford the cost of a motor van, or wish to buy it? Most butchers were sportsmen, as were innkeepers and auctioneers and other men in business in a modest way for themselves. They loved horses and understood them, and so did the farmer. They would not wish to learn about the workings of the motor when they could set themselves up with a smart cart and a cob.

Rich men liked motor cars. But, Mr Richardson asserted, they kept horses as well. They raced and hunted and played polo, even if they travelled in an automobile between these activities. He was confident that the horse would prosper in the future.

He was wrong. He had chosen to ignore signs all around him in his desire to halt the tide of history. If the steam ploughs had failed to take over from the horse in most cases, then the steam thresher had become universal in its use. Although the Army continued to see the cavalry as its finest possession, it was busy examining the possible use of military ambulances, lorries and supply trucks. They were also interested in the performance of mechanical transport of a different kind. Orville and Wright flew in the air in 1903 with propulsion from a petrol engine, and aviation races were held in Doncaster in 1909. The military capabilities of the aeroplane were soon to become tragically obvious, while the inadequacy of the cavalry horse to cope with modern warfare was a sickening surprise for those generals who had failed to realize, like Mr Richardson before them, that the horse had no practical role in twentieth-century military life.

Among the first to recognize the trends of the times were showmen. Their livelihood depended on supplying their public with the latest novelty, and they had made significant changes to their roundabouts of horses and carriages years before Mr Richardson wrote his book proclaiming the future of the horse. Roundabouts had been a feature of country fairs for hundreds of years. In the early days, turned by ponies, they were sedate rides for the unadventurous. With the arrival of steam engines, the showmen, quick on the uptake as usual, immediately saw the advantages of adapting the merry-go-round to steam. They constructed the machines so that the engine was housed

The semi-invalid artist Frances Jennings loved her donkey companion, Eva, and wrote about her exploits in letters to friends. Frances found that her evening fires often attracted local people who came to talk to her and give her presents of fruit and bread.

A good-looking horse attracted the admiration of men from every station in life.

in a truck in the centre, while the 'ride' itself consisted of a rotating frame, or 'spinning top', with different types of carriages suspended from it. One builder of these roundabouts, Frederick Savage of King's Lynn, in Norfolk, became the undisputed master of the craft, and his shop produced exquisitely decorated rides of great and varied complexity and beauty. After the 1890s, there was sufficient business in the carving and decoration of roundabouts and biograph booths to keep firms in full-time business. These workers, who would also have painted the showmen's caravans in elaborate colours, portrayed fantastic scenes which covered most of the roundabout, from the spinning top to the special truck that stood inside the ride, with the engine truck, and which housed the organ. This was built in the shape of a gondola, was lavishly painted, and ran on its own rubber wheels. The carriages, which were suspended from the spinning-top frame, were originally static, so the rider simply swirled round to the sound of organ music. Then overhead cranks were added, to operate poles that were called 'horse rods'. These were attached to the frame at one end and to the carriage at the other, and enabled the rider to move up and down at the same time as he went round. By far the most popular rides when the steam merry-go-rounds were in full swing were those with fancy carved horses. The ordinary people loved to gallop round on a mare with a flowing mane, or to imagine themselves on a hunter like a squire. But in the first few years of the twentieth century the popularity of the horse rides plummeted. Wise roundabout operators removed the horses and replaced them with dummy cars, complete with fake rubber wheels. These were hugely successful until after the end of the First World War. When the public ceased to find them a novelty, in the 1920s, their taste did not revert to the old carved horses of earlier days. Instead they craved bizarre transport for their amusement, like dragons and peacocks. It was only decades later, when horses were seen as relics of the past, that the fairground operators resurrected the chargers and hunters and found an enthusiastic audience for them.

The showmen had pulled the rides from one show to the next without the use of horses in most cases since the turn of the century. The caravans were pulled, sometimes in a string six or seven vans long, by one steam-engine. So long as there was water handy to fill the boiler at regular intervals, the showman could move around with comparative ease.

These men had in fact adapted to the trends and mechanical devices of the first decade of the twentieth century far more quickly and successfully than the Establishment, who found it harder to absorb new ideas and jealously guarded the horse as a symbol of upper-class privilege. King Edward VII predicted, when he was still a prince and had just taken his first ride in a motor car, that all gentlemen would eventually own a car. All gentlemen already owned a horse, and they were in no hurry to part with it, so long as there was a plentiful supply of grooms and stableboys to attend its needs. The horse held a special place in the affection and was cherished and maintained despite its cost, because it was beautiful to watch, intelligent and well-mannered, and all refined people considered it to be their rightful 'partner in civilization'.

CHAPTER 9

THE CARAVAN CLUB

On 5 April 1907, the advertising magazine *Bazaar, Exchange and Mart* included in its column devoted to sports and pastimes under the regular listing for caravanning the following items:

First-class private touring caravan, in perfect condition, every convenience, commodious, light, suited for one horse. Price moderate. For particulars apply (Sussex).
Gipsy touring van for sale, just done up, ready for immediate use (Surrey).
Pleasure caravan required, no rubbish, fully equipped. McIntire, High Wells, Kendal.
Wanted, gentleman's travelling caravan (with motor preferred) in exchange for 10 h.p. Lanchester motor car, seat 5, cost £500. 21, Burton-rd, Derby.
To gentlemen tourists. Capital light American touring van, by Mills, with waterproof canvas top, front and back curtains, extension tent, spring mattresses, table and racks, equal to new. Cost 60gs. accept 28gs. Lester, Aylesbury.

This list covered the whole variety of caravans then available for the enthusiast, except for the heavy, two-horse version first favoured by rich bohemians but now rapidly falling out of style. However, a few examples still appeared, built by wealthy eccentrics. The most notable of these was the 'Comet', made in 1906 for the French nobleman the Baron de Sennevoy. His 'home car' included quarters for two domestics, who had their own servants' entrance at the front of the caravan. There was a plug-in phone, and a piano and American portable organ for the Baroness to play. The walls were double-panelled to provide insulation against heat and cold and the whole contraption weighed a massive amount. One account put it as high as seven tons, and it is doubtful that it ever moved much in its life. This degree of luxury and ostentatious expense was very much against the modern trend. Great efforts were made by authors of articles about caravanning to convince the public that the pastime need not be expensive. Every piece of literature on the subject during the first two decades of the century seemed to include a list of expenses (always extraordinarily reasonable) incurred by an average party on tour. The most provident of them all was Lady Arthur Grosvenor, who

reckoned, in her contribution to *The Camper's Handbook*, that the cost was as
little as five shillings and a halfpenny per person per day. This figure was so
low that J. Harris Stone in his book *Caravanning and Camping Out* felt bound to
mention that he spent considerably more than that amount when he went
travelling. The ability to live on next to nothing in a caravan became quite
fashionable, and it is possible to imagine middle-class men and women
desperately paring down their diet to minimal amounts of porridge and stew
in order that they might claim, on their return to civilization, that they had
survived on less than anyone else had yet achieved. When Dugald Semple
moved into his omnibus in the woods in order to follow the Simple Life he
became quite famous after extensive press coverage of the 'Linwood Hermit',
or the 'Vegetablearian'. People flocked to visit his bus and to stare at him. As
they swarmed around, poking at his few belongings, their inevitable question
was about the economics of his venture. Just how little could be survive on?
Mr Semple managed on five shillings a week, but he ate no meat or dairy

*'The Caravan Craze – scene in a lonely part of the Highlands.' George Morrow commemorated the
sudden surge of interest in leisure caravanning in a 1908* Punch *cartoon.*

products because of his philosophical beliefs, and subsisted on a diet that consisted entirely of pulses, nuts and fruits. In the book he wrote in his caravan, *Life in the Open*, he emphasized that a van 'needn't be the palace on wheels of the wealthy globe-trotter nor the carved edifice of the gentleman gypsy.' In their enthusiasm to dispel the fear of the public that you needed to be a millionaire to take a caravan tour, the adherents of the pastime came in danger of convincing their readers that a trip was at best a health cure and at worst an endurance test, guaranteed to bring the intrepid explorer back weighing considerably less than he did when he set off.

Plenty of recipes were published for the meals that a caravanner should eat whilst out in the open air. Most of these were made up of solid, 'healthy' ingredients. Pleasure travellers got plenty of roughage in their diet. Dugald Semple, whose wife also published recipe books, eventually became the Secretary of the London Vegetarian Society, and spent the war years touring round giving lectures on food economy, a subject in which he had gathered plenty of personal experience during his caravan days. L.C.R. Cameron finished his book, *The Book of the Caravan*, with a chapter on living from the natural products of the land. He included recipes for snail soup (two dozen snails to a pint of water), hedgehog with sorrel or watercress sauce, and dormouse with poppy-seed and honey. He did not claim to have personally eaten all the food he recommended, but he was very enthusiastic about the stems of the great reed which can be cooked and eaten like asparagus, and the sprouts of the hawthorn that can be taken raw. His breakdown of costs for travel, which presumably included a diet supplemented by free nettle soup and crystallized primroses, was at the rate of £2 for a week on the road for two. This did not include the rental cost of the van.

These varied enormously in price, whether they were bought or rented. It was partly in order to make available a list of reasonable and well maintained caravans for hire that J. Harris Stone, writer and barrister, gathered ten people together at his house on 14 June 1907 to form the Caravan Club of Great Britain and Ireland. Their goal was 'to bring together those interested in van-life as a pastime', and the annual subscription was set at 5 shillings. The founder members were an enlightened group, so they agreed that ladies should be eligible to join the club by election, in just the same way that gentlemen were. Dr W. Gordon Stables was chosen as Vice-President of the Club, but he was an old and sick man by then, and took little active interest in the proceedings. He died in 1910, leaving his caravan, the 'Wanderer', to be auctioned off. Harris Stone had hoped that a museum would buy it, but there was no money forthcoming, and it was eventually purchased by members of Stables' own family. Finally it ended up in the City Museum, Bristol, where it can still be viewed.

The club, even without the figurehead of the grand old man of caravanning, prospered. By 1913 there were three hundred members, a third of whom were women. Mr Stone was pleased by this. He had opened *Caravanning and Camping Out* with a discussion on the physique of twentieth-century women, who, he was delighted to note, had bigger bones, deeper chests, squarer shoulders and stronger hands than their Victorian grandmothers. He attributed this change to sport. Alpine holidays spent climbing and skating, or holidays on bicycles, yachting trips and rounds of golf all helped to make girls grow up into strapping women. They enjoyed new freedom in everyday life as well. Unlike their grandmothers, they queued for buses, hailed taxi-cabs on their own, lived like bachelors in flats, and even went on caravan holidays without the help of husbands or male servants. Like the three ladies in *Bealby, A Holiday* by H.G. Wells, they went travelling with a 'breezy freedom' which, even if it did mostly consist of washing up and an 'anxious quest' for the next camp-site, also allowed them the luxury of thinking for themselves, without deferring to their husbands' opinions for a while. The character Judy Bowles, squatting in a short brown skirt, a deerstalker hat, a large white apron and

Mr Mallalieu's van was considered the first practical motor caravan to be used in Great Britain.

splatterdashes over her pan of frying onions, bacon and potatoes, is a contented woman. Her two companions are happy, too, as they sit sprawled in the grass to eat their meal, free of all lady-like constraints. H.G. Wells pokes gentle fun at them, showing that they soon tire of the pleasure of the open-air life and long to get back to hotels and golf courses with their husbands; but before they return to their more conventional life they have had enormous enjoyment from a freer existence and the simple entertainments offered by a show by some passing travelling players, or a quiet conversation round the firelight.

The lady caravanners of real life were a formidable group. Dressed, as recommended in *Caravanning and Camping Out*, in a thick walking skirt (with a linen one packed away for really hot weather), they pulled their shady hats down low against the driving rain and set out in groups, or alone, with a bold independence. Several of them owned their own transport. Miss Simmons had a van called the 'Tally-Ho', which had originally belonged to a showman and still retained its interior decoration from that time. She travelled with two lady companions, cooked their meals under a waterproof canvas annexe, and took them wherever hunting, shooting and fishing were plentiful.

Mrs Towers went on tour with her two bob-tail sheepdogs, for whom she had created a double kennel underneath the van. The two dogs lay in a canvas tube that ran from rear to front of the undercarriage, and which was hung with curtains in front to keep the kennels warm and dry even in the rain. Both dogs knew exactly how to push their curtains aside when they disappeared for a nap.

Miss Charlotte L. Sheppard, an artist, had lived for some ten years previously on a Nile boat; so when she came to have a caravan made for her she modelled it on the same lines as her boat, and named it 'Egypt'. At 16 feet in length, and 6½ feet in width, fixed on very low wheels, it was one of the few caravans that could successfully travel on a train. Its centre height inside was six feet, and there were two berths at the rear, 6 feet by 2 feet 4 inches, with netted racks above for belongings, like those found on board a ship. A hostess stove heated the saloon and was used for cooking. There were no partitions, so the whole interior formed a large, sparsely furnished studio.

Another artist, Frances Jennings, travelled in a much humbler van. She had collapsed with an acute attack of myelitis at the age of 23 which left her left leg paralysed. She was an orphan, and penniless, so a group of six women friends undertook to pay her expenses for the rest of her life. At her request they bought her a converted coster's barrow and a donkey from the East End of London, and in this she travelled alone. At first she was often worried by policemen and frightened by the gypsies she met on the road, but after she had joined the Caravan Club and discovered where it was safe to pitch at night, and had built up a network of acquaintances who were prepared to let her camp in a paddock or piece of their garden, she managed better. She was a woman with an elfish quality about her, who lived slightly apart from the rest of the world even before her illness, and she had always chosen to keep very much to herself. The caravan gave her some of the freedom back that she had lost with her disability, and although she was often lonely and afraid, she loved camp life and her van. 'What a nice possession a little blue wooden wagon is, with a white hood,' she wrote to a friend. 'A thing like that gives one a certain small power in the world, and means of making friendships and delighting people, and is a charm.' About her evening fires, she wrote, 'My furnaces! and blazes! and growing heaps! are my stocks in trade. I find, if I light a great beautiful fire, the village people, almost without fail, come and herd around, and the inhabitants of the houses come attracted out, and more often than not, they dance and sing.'

In December, in 1912, she was still out, camping alone in the freezing weather. The doctors had told her that she needed fresh air to keep in reasonable health, but many people were afraid that the winter cold would be more than she could stand. At that time she wrote to Harris Stone, who had become a friend of hers, saying, 'I find great excitement in the winter, in hearing the storms raving around me in the black of night. I have spent a few nights with poor travellers at the roadside and shared their supper – rabbit and cabbage and potatoes. They have spoken like poets, worn silver rings on their copper hands, and rosy beads around their necks; and their babies have round little twigs of hazel-nuts in their red hands. And perhaps the roof of their cart has been on the sea – the sail of a ship.'

She eventually came back to Chelsea to live, but she was horribly restricted by her disease. She lived on the floor, crawling between cushions. A friend who visited her in a room she had for a while in Cheyne Walk, Chelsea, found her sitting on the ground, hacking open a tin of condensed milk with a bill-hook. She was dressed in sacking (she made all her own dresses out of sacking and then painted them with blue designs) and had an emerald cap shoved on her head to disguise the fact that she had chopped off her long fair hair. As her health failed, she grew increasingly melancholy. Her rather Nordic beauty faded, and she wrote, 'I am a dying thing.' Eventually she killed herself, in October 1915. She left behind some fine drawings, and letters full of the beauty of the countryside and the different ways of people whom she had encountered as she travelled. Proud and vulnerable, she went about alone with great courage, and tried to take the most she could from the appalling situation in which she found herself. The odds against her were too great. She wrote, 'It was as paradise, only I was alone.'

Another woman, Miss Whistler, won the prize offered in 1907 for the design for the Club Pennon. She composed a design with two Cs entwined back to back on a horse-shoe. Many members of the committee were horrified.

'Horse-shoe! why, vans may all become motor vans some day, and the horse-shoe will then be merely an historic relic,' they protested. The horse-shoe on the pennon was changed to a V on the grounds that, whether horse- or motor-drawn, there would always be a van involved.

The indignation of the club members was odd, since all of them were strongly opposed to motor caravans, and although they tolerated their owners as members they regarded the whole idea of motor travel as something outside the spirit of true caravanning. At the Club's annual dinner of 1912, Sir Henry Rider Haggard, the author, who had caravanned in Africa in a vehicle drawn by oxen, spoke against those who 'were trying to cram into a day what they should do in a week.' Harris Stone was quite rude about motor caravanners in *Caravanning and Camping Out*. Since the vehicles were so heavy it was hard to park anywhere but in the yard of a first-class hotel. The wheels would sink deeply into the grass, and the bodies of most motor caravans were so long that they could not be turned round in any sort of confined space. Since Mr Stone considered that most owners of motor caravans wanted only

Mr F. Geoffrey Smith's van (interior, looking aft), with its bunks. There were many experiments with the positioning of beds in the early pleasure caravans.

to get from one good hotel to another as fast as possible, so that they could eat their meals in the hotel dining-rooms, he did not think it mattered to them that they only saw the countryside as a blur as they raced from breakfast in one town to lunch in the next. He related with scorn his meeting with a motor caravanner who boasted that he could 'do' ninety miles a day. This man carried a capable chef and had a first-rate wine cellar. A winding staircase from inside the body of the car connected it to the roof, where easy chairs were placed. The party reclined on these as they travelled, so that they could see the scenery as they drove along.

Mr Stone was slightly less critical of the members of the Caravan Club who had motor vans. He described the one belonging to Mr J.W. Mallalieu of Wavertree, Liverpool, as the first practical motor caravan in Britain. The French had been using them for some time. Mr Mallalieu's van was referred to by many writers of the time, but it was never mentioned by name. This is perhaps significant. Names were very important to the owners of horse-drawn caravans. They dreamt up sobriquets such as Escargot, Brunnhilde, Sunlight, Tally-Ho, Maisonette, Triumvir, Lady-go-Lightly, Pathfinder, the Bohemian, and dozens more like them, each one chosen to sum up for the owner his own special brand of adventure and abandonment. Mr Mallalieu may not have wanted to feel these things. He could have simply wanted a practical means of transport to take him and his family to nice places where they could sleep in comfort out of doors, if they wished to do so. He would not have

Lady Carbery's 'nest of beds' for economizing on space. The amateur designers of caravans, who were all practising enthusiastis, often came up with the best ideas for innovations, which they shared with each other at the meetings of the Caravan Club.

needed a name for a vehicle that merely moved him from A to B and the next beauty spot for camping. He had plenty of room in his van, which had space for six beds. It was long, 21 feet 9 inches, the standard width of 6 feet and 6 inches, and it weighed 4 tons when fully laden. It averaged only nine miles an hour as it lumbered along, so the Mallalieu family, at least, must have seen something more than a flash and a blur of the countryside as they travelled towards the next first-class hotel.

Miss Simmons and friends took their van, the 'Tally Ho', wherever the hunting, shooting and fishing were plentiful.

Another member, Mrs Paton, did name her motor caravan, which was built in 1912. Called the 'Tortoise', it was nearly square in shape. Luggage lived on the top and was reached by a movable ladder. The driver's seat could convert into a bunk for one. The body of the car contained a dining room with an anthracite stove and a bedroom with two bunks set along the offside wall and chest of drawers and cupboards ranged round the rest of the room.

The Motor Show at Olympia in 1909 featured the Austin Caravan, a sumptuous contraption designed to carry, feed and sleep four people, including the chef and chauffeur, and intended only for very rich people indeed. It was a more compact vehicle than Mr Mallalieu's car, being only 12 feet 3 inches long and 6 feet 6 inches wide. The dining-room could seat six, in case its owners wished to entertain in the van. The sitting-room contained sleeping arrangements and was richly decorated with inlaid mahogany panels. The ceiling was of satinwood and a clerestory roof gave plenty of light and headroom. Two tanks on the roof supplied water to the fully fitted lavatory and to the kitchen. A serving window separated the kitchen quarters from the saloon, and the servants slept in two bunks on the roof that were cleverly disguised by day as a large travelling trunk. When opened, it revealed a complete bed in either half, which could be covered with a canvas awning if necessary. Telephone communication between the compartments and the driver was included in the price of £2,000. The van weighed 2½ tons, and would certainly have spent most of its time parked in the inn yard. Although it was superbly made of English ash, with exterior panels of aluminium sheeting to lessen the overall weight, and fine craftsmanship and clever design could be found in each detail of its manufacture, it was, as L.C.R. Cameron would have been quick to point out, a 'white elephant'. The future of motor caravans really lay in their curiosity value, and as luxurious gimmicks for the men who had everything. The horse-drawn equivalents, like that of the showman Lord George Sanger which featured a massive carved chimney-piece, were also disappearing fast. The rich and ostentatious who wanted vans at all favoured those with motors. When the Gaekwar of Baroda and the Maharajah of Gwalior arrived at the 1911 Meet of the Caravan Club in a fleet of royal cars to look over the possible permutations of vans to take home with them, it was the motor caravans that they decided to buy. The van finally designed for the Maharajah of Gwalior was for use by himself and his guests while big-game hunting, but the emphasis was on luxury rather than mobility. It could sleep sixteen people in all comfort, and in fact consisted of a motor van with a trailer attachment behind.

The trailer caravan had barely been considered. Harris Stone mentioned in passing, in *Caravanning and Camping Out*, an ingenious new way of overcoming the problems of the motor caravan which had recently come to his notice. The owner of a small two-seater car had fixed an iron bar to the front of his

Mrs Paton's 'Tortoise', which was motor-driven, contained a dining-room fitted with an anthracite stove.

Many caravans sported canvas sun-shades, which protected the paintwork in the hot sun and provided insulation against the heat.

caravan, which 'can be attached by a simple contrivance to the back of the motor carriage, which then draws the van at the rate of some five or six miles an hour'. The motor car could then be detached at the pitch and used for outings. Mr Stone thought that the idea might be bright enough to be imitated by others.

This was, in fact, how most innovations developed; from discussions that the caravanners had together over the difficulties that they had encountered and the methods they had used to overcome the problems. Most professional builders were wheelwrights and coachbuilders, who were carrying on a tradition of craftsmanship developed when carriages required sturdy materials and solid frames to withstand the terrible roads of the early nineteenth century. They found it difficult to adapt to the new demand for lightweight touring boxes. The people who really knew what was needed were the caravanners themselves, and the best new vans were all built to their designs and specifications. The caravan meets held annually were partly so that members could inspect the new concepts expressed in each others' vans, and there was a strong spirit of co-operation amongst the members.

Bertram Smith had already pioneered the idea of light, easily manoeuvrable vans, and other enthusiasts had been working on their own theories about ways of streamlining their vehicles. Double-skinned vans, with felted roofs, provided the best insulation against the cold and heat, but they weighed more than the single-skinned variety. A sun cloth, hung over the van in the hot weather, would work well for summer travellers, and make a second skin unnecessary. Since most people only travelled in the good months of the year in any case, most van-owners dispensed with stoves altogether and relied either on a primus stove or a camp-fire, using an iron crane, as recommended by Lady Arthur Grosvenor, from which to hang their cooking-pot.

The food reform shopowner Bertram Hutchings, who had not yet given up his shop entirely in favour of the caravan business, had built himself a most compact and lightweight van and named it the 'Maisonette'. The interior was small, only 6 feet 4 inches by 4 feet 6 inches, with beds running one above the other along the entire length of the offside wall. The front of the wall was hinged, and dropped down at the pitch to be supported by two slender posts so that it could form a 6-foot extension. This could be used as a large table; alternatively, at night, when enclosed with an awning, it made an extra sleeping compartment. While travelling, the upper half of the hinged front folded down so that the driver could direct his pony from his seat inside the van. The whole weighed only 8 hundredweight, which made it wonderfully manoeuvrable. It also contained a feature new to caravans: a portable shower. This consisted of a hose with a brush on the end through which water sprayed, and it was much admired by Hutchings' fellow Simple Lifer Dugald Semple, the 'Linwood Hermit'.

The Lady-go-Lightly, a one-chamber, one-horse van which was used by the Bishop of Stepney when he travelled each year to Kent to visit the hop-pickers, was considered a particularly well-designed vehicle. It was sparsely furnished, but contained drawers cleverly made to conceal documents and valuables. Several of the vans had similar arrangements, because although the travellers were glad to live in an unconventional manner on their tours, they did occasionally like to rejoin civilization, put on their jewellery, and have a slap-up meal in a local hotel. They also needed to carry some money in case of disaster, so they took the sensible precaution of building in secret stashing places.

The interiors of the caravans were changing their appearance rapidly as people moved away from the rigid floor-plan dictated by a standard gypsy or showman's van. Once again, it was the amateurs who came up with new ideas. Sir James Moody, the Club President, and an eminent brain specialist, who often recommended caravanning to patients suffering from overwork, stress or total breakdown on the grounds that it offered 'complete brain rest', designed a sleeping-berth settee: a sofa by day, which a simple movement converted into two berths in the evening. Lady Carbery invented a system for stowing away three beds on one wall. A spring bed which rested on two brackets was fixed to the end wall. Beneath this, two similar beds on strong, light castors, each slightly smaller than the last, fitted together rather like a nest of tables in the drawing-room. The blankets were stored on top of the fixed bed, which had a cretonne cover that reached to the floor, and this served as a comfortable and attractive couch during the day. In Geoffrey Smith's Rolling Stone the bunks were all fixed on the rear wall, one above the other, while in the Pathfinder, a strange van which ran on only three wheels, a man's bunk could be let down on chains on the outside wall, so that the servant could sleep in privacy, away from the main party, and then put away his bed in the morning before setting off on the next day's journey.

Almost everything in the caravans folded. Pantry doors, hinged at the bottom instead of the side, folded down to make tables; combined baths and washstands made of green rotproof canvas that folded up and weighed only seven pounds could be purchased from the Army and Navy Stores; even latrine seats could be folded after use. Beds turned into chairs and sideboards into beds. Some people used their ingenuity to create the impossible, like Johnston Green of Birkdale, who designed his van, 'Halcyon', so that the ladies and gentlemen on the expedition could enjoy complete privacy, women at one end, men at the other, and would never need to pass through each other's apartments. Others, like Matthew Arnold, contributor to the *Camper's Handbook*, preferred to solve the problem of privacy with brilliant simplicity. His party carried a twenty-yard-long roll of unbleached calico, which could be wound round four upright poles to form a bathing tent for the ladies at the

J. Harris Stone founded the Caravan Club in 1907 in order to bring together 'like-minded people interested in van-life as a pastime'.

appropriate time. At night, it was erected by the caravan to serve as a windshield while the campers lolled in hammock chairs beside the fire.

Enthusiasm was high. Each year the numbers grew at the Caravan Club Meets. Attended by a detachment of Boy Scouts who acted as guards and amateur firemen, always ready with buckets of water in case of fire, the members circulated. They peered at each other's improvements and collected more information for the register of pitches: places where farmers were known to be prepared to take in Caravan Club members to their fields. They swapped stories and read articles about the hobby that gave them so much pleasure. One Caravan Club member, Leonard Richmond, was so enthralled with his caravan, the Arcadian, that he decided to drive in it from the church after his wedding, and to stay in it for the rest of his honeymoon. He married his cousin, Elsie, who also loved travelling, and between them they owned three vans, two gypsy *vardos* and the saloon version that they used on honeymoon. It was luxuriously fitted and probably made a very comfortable bridal suite. It contained a Dulcitone, a piano that produced its sound when the pads struck tuning forks. Mrs Richmond was a very accomplished singer, and in the long evenings she would often delight guests by sitting at the piano, lit by the newly installed electric light, and singing songs to her own accompaniment.

All these caravans were built for pleasure. None of the Caravan Club members would have dreamed of spending all year inside their vans, battling with the folding bath and studying the *Contour Road Book* to discover when they could expect the next hill too steep for Dobbin to climb without help from a tracer horse borrowed from a local farmer. They went for relaxation, to indulge in their hobbies. They collected butterflies and antiques and walked their dogs over the moors, then came home to their comfortable houses to tell stories for the rest of the year about their adventures. Their sole motive in travelling the roads in a caravan was the pursuit of pleasure.

CHAPTER 10

CARAVANS FOR LIVING

The people who did stay in vans all the year round were too poor to afford the luxuries of even the simplest pleasure caravans. They were mostly, apart from the gypsies and tinkers who had taken to vans as a natural part of their nomadic lifestyle, social reformers of one sort or another, whose reasons for existing on the fringes of society were dictated by their own personal philosophies. They lived very much from hand to mouth. Even the 'Linwood Hermit', Dugald Semple, admitted that only men with strong convictions, and often extremists, managed to survive on the road, because it was so hard for them to earn enough to eat. It was often easier to make a fortune in the cities than to sustain life in the countryside, where jobs, even of the itinerant variety, were scarce. Some serious Simple Life adherents lived in caravans on smallholdings. The athlete George H. Allen, who had been born sickly but had managed to overcome his poor health and become a champion walker, supported a household of six on his three acres of land. He was an ardent vegetarian, and he had a grim determination to survive, but he was exceptional in his success. Very few people could manage to make a go of such an enterprise.

Dugald Semple supported himself for some time as an engineer in the nearby town after he had made camp in the woods in his old omnibus; later he cut himself completely free from normal employment and started to write and lecture as a means of earning his living. He decided to move out into the country in order to get away from the scourge of the city. He considered that man had become enslaved, not freed, by science, and he passionately espoused the causes of Socialism and the redistribution of land. Like the man in the novel *The Yellow Van* he went about preaching, 'People for the land and land for the People'. In his books he mourned the loss of thousands of acres of arable land during the first years of the century, abandoned by an increasingly urban society. He believed that Britain could and should feed herself, if properly managed. While half a dozen families owned half of Scotland and laws were designed to protect the privileged classes, he saw no hope for the revitalization of the country, but he hoped for a redistribution of power in which socialist co-operatives could till the land, without the use of chemicals, to produce a good vegetarian diet for all.

He attracted a lot of attention. Sitting in his omnibus, which he liked because the twelve windows provided a lot of light and made it possible to sunbathe in bed, he drew large crowds. His advice on health and diet was consistent with most of the alternative doctrines put forward by doctors outside the mainstream of medical opinion at the turn of the century. Fresh air and sunlight still topped the bill as health-giving substances. Ozone was good. Meat could produce an excess of uric acid in the body and lead to appendicitis, gout, rheumatism, arthritis and cancer. He was more controversial on the subject of love. Semple was originally drawn to the idea of celibacy, but concluded that sex was a necessary function, like eating. He was no supporter of suffragettes, and was furious when a prankster wrote 'Votes for Women' in paint and tar on either side of his caravan horse while he attended the Glasgow Fair in 1913. He thought that women should marry only when they had enough money of their own to make them independent of their husbands, but he considered their position little better than that of slaves otherwise. He felt that they should worry less about the unimportant issue of the vote and more about the desirability of women ruling in the home. He also advocated free divorce. These ideas were quite revolutionary for the time, although politicians were gradually coming to the opinion that marriage contracts were unnecessarily harsh for women and that they should be allowed property rights, even if they were not yet ready to deal responsibly with the vote.

When Dugald Semple married, he chose a partner who fitted in with his beliefs. Cathie Semple was a vegetarian, and she was independently rich, as the Glasgow *Evening Times and News* rather cattily impressed upon its readers in its coverage of the ceremony: 'Mr Dugald Semple, the well-known simple lifer, author, and health lecturer, was married in Glasgow yesterday to a charming Kilmacolm widow, the owner of a large house and grounds.'

By now Dugald Semple had built his own van, of the showman's type, with strong ribbed sides, and he was employed by the London Vegetarian Society, so he had achieved a certain degree of respectability. He still, however, had rather wilder friends, who roamed the countryside, or set up craftsmen's guilds on isolated smallholdings. One such friend, a Welsh former aeronaut, built himself a van and travelled the land flying the rainbow flag of World Brotherhood. He supported himself by doing odd jobs of vulcanizing or electro-plating in the towns and villages he passed.

If he had taken down his flag and ceased to proselytize, conducted his craft in a serious manner and allowed market forces to dictate how long he remained in each place, he would have been leading the sort of life that Harris Stone had advocated in *Caravanning and Camping Out* as a way of solving some

Dugald Semple was furious when a prankster painted 'votes for women' on the side of his horse while he was on a lecture tour. He was not a supporter of Mrs Pankhurst.

of the problems of society. He was no socialist reformer, but he did hope that a large new section of caravanners would appear. Between the pleasure caravans and the gypsy *vardos*, he believed that there was room for another class of traveller. Since the towns were rapidly becoming unbearable through overcrowding and pollution, he hoped that craftsmen and artisans would better their lives by taking their families with them and embarking on a caravan existence. He expected them to move from town to town, staying for as long as business prevailed, then to travel on to the next place for a few weeks or months. He saw dentists, upholsterers, sign-makers, clock- and watch-menders and dealers in antiques all on the move.

His vision was shared by a man called Basil A. Slade, who invented a new kind of caravan called a 'vancott'. This was designed to fulfil a 'far-reaching political motive in housing country labourers'. It consisted of five rooms, plus a little pantry and water-closet, and allowed for a parlour 14 feet 6 inches long, with a headroom of 6 feet 8 inches. This miniature two-storeyed cottage stood on an oblong braced iron frame and two artillery wheels. The forepart

Dugald Semple's spartan lifestyle and controversial views on marriage, money and politics fascinated the public.

of the frame was V-shaped, and it had a coupling arm for attachment to a horse or engine. The cottage sat on a wheel base that was only 8 feet long and then overhung it to a width of 11 feet. The dwelling could be constructed cheaply, to sell, including the iron wheels, at £85.

A photograph of the vancott shows a rather pretty half-timbered cottage in the shape of a gingerbread house drawn by two fine carthorses down a country lane. The proportions of the cottage were probably generous compared with the conditions suffered by many farm labourers of the time, who lived in miserable tithed hovels. But the idea of the vancott never caught on. Perhaps, however unpleasant the conditions at home, it was better to belong somewhere than to roam from job to job without friends or family

The 'vancott', or movable cottage. Basil A. Slade hoped his vancott would answer the housing needs of labourers, but the idea never caught on.

around to give support when times were bad. Most people did not want to live like gypsies. They liked coming home to the same place to go to bed at night. From the rich bourgeoisie, who hired their caravans from Fortnum & Mason, or Harrods, or Whiteleys to dabble in luxurious bohemianism for a few days, to the poor cottager who had no knowledge of the world twenty miles from his home village, there was a basic shared conservatism that kept people firmly rooted to the spot where they felt that they belonged. The pleasure for the middle- and upper-class travellers came precisely from the novelty of an experience so different from their solid, safe, respectable life, where everyone knew them by name and nothing changed from year to year.

The Edwardian era, seen with hindsight as the last sunny afternoon of an innocent world before the horror of the First World War changed the face of civilization, was in fact a time full of uneasy confusion. One of the attractions of the caravan for many was that it was a step away from the new fast world of cars and planes. The middle classes had stayed essentially Victorian in their views, in order to cope better with the increasing barrage of new sensations that science and technology introduced. They resisted the theories of Sigmund Freud about the forbidden subject of sex, and they refused to delve into their unconscious minds. They preferred the charming plays and novels of Somerset Maugham and Compton Mackenzie to those of D.H. Lawrence and the popular but controversial George Bernard Shaw (the latter was, incidentally, a great believer in Dr Jaeger's Sanitary Woollen System). They bought nice, pretty pictures to hang on their walls, and joined in the noisy condemnation of the pictures chosen by the artist Roger Fry for an exhibition at the Grafton Gallery in 1910. The paintings by Gauguin, Matisse, Picasso and other Post-Impressionist painters provoked furious discussion. Most people feared and hated their formlessness, in the same way that they disliked the new books that burrowed deep into the inner motivations of their characters instead of getting on with the plot, and the new ballets and symphonies that seemed to have no good tunes in them. The feeling increased with each passing year that things were happening that they did not fully understand, and that despite a united stand for the past, life was slipping out of control. The same feeling prevailed in politics, and particularly in foreign affairs. For some time there had been a war brewing. Naval competition with Germany became more intense after the turn of the century. The ultimate warship, the *Dreadnought*, was built in 1906 as an unmistakable message to the Germans that the British were so far ahead in technology that war was out of the question. Like all deterrents, it failed in its objective. The Germans built faster, improving their fleet with aggressive deliberation. The people knew that they could do nothing to stop the inevitable. They were moved helplessly along, like a stick in the current, towards the weir of destruction.

At home, behaviour grew worse. Women ran amok in the streets, throwing bombs in their pursuit of the vote. The People's Budget introduced Old Age Pensions, which many sections of society were convinced would soon bankrupt the country. Then came the cruellest blow of all, when the goddess of modern technology, the great liner *Titanic*, sank on its maiden voyage. The newspapers chronicled it all with shrill headlines. Lord Northcliffe now owned the *Daily Mirror*, the *Daily Mail* and the prestigious *Times*. He was a brilliant entrepreneur who could manufacture news if none had arrived legitimately for the morning editions. He gave the new reading public the stories they wanted to hear. They revelled in society divorce cases, articles about the latest dance crazes – and the exploits of the Grosvenors in their caravan at Ascot. Everyone busied themselves in following the gossip, keeping in fashion, and spending their money on all the consumer products that the newspaper advertisements promised them would make life easier, and pleasanter, and take away their uneasy fears. While they indulged in fads to keep their minds occupied, they clung on to the things that they knew, and the traditions that had kept them safe all through the long, successful reign of Queen Victoria.

The tradesmen who had been expected to take to their caravans and live the free existence of nomads were never likely to look kindly on the idea. They came from a background of businesses handed down from father to son, and of reputations built from painstaking years of meticulous service to a community. They were even less inclined to think of such options in the last years before the Great War. They had no need to change their own lives. World events were about to rearrange them anyway. Like the rest of their countrymen, they waited with bated breath for the moment to arrive. Before a thunderstorm the air is so unbearable that it is almost a relief when the first streak of lightning cuts the sky. It must have felt a lot like that in Britain in August 1914.

CHAPTER 11

WAR AND AFTER

The First World War changed everything. Whether people went to the Front or stayed at home, they were never going to return to the peaceful life that they knew before 1914. They did not realize this immediately. Although some soldiers warned that the war might last for a long time (General Kitchener took the especially grim view that it could take three years to beat the Germans) most people expected it to be 'all over by Christmas'. Caught up in the exhilaration that nations experience when they first go into battle, and secure in the belief that modern methods of warfare made a long encounter impossible, the British enlisted in great numbers and marched off to the sound of the military bands. *Punch*, in 1914, branded Germany as the 'Mad Dog of Europe' and reminded its readers of the famous quotation from Oliver Goldsmith: 'The man recovered from the bite. The dog it was that died.'

This mood of pugnacious optimism remained strong despite the terrible tragedies of the next year. Even after the shock of the sinking of the British liner the *Lusitania*, with the loss of 1,200 lives, people remained cheerful. Maimed soldiers back from the Front arrived in their droves at the railway stations and gave the civilians their first real confrontation with the consequences of the war. These men kept their faith with the mood of the times and cracked jokes with their nurses about their horrific wounds. Soldiers who survived in the trenches kept up their spirits with a uniquely British brand of black comedy. When the November rains turned the fields of Flanders into a sea of mud, a soldier wrote home to England that 'trench warfare is becoming a constant drain'.[7]

More money and more men were constantly needed at the Front, and the civilians who were left behind increasingly took over the jobs that fell vacant in the factories and fields. Women did work that had always been considered suitable only for men. They became ticket-collectors, bank clerks, munitions-makers and postwomen. As many as possible crossed to the continent to work as nurses and drivers, and those who could not go tried to contribute whatever they could in aid of the war effort. As the years passed they left behind the traditionally passive role of mothers and wives who knitted socks and wrote cheerful letters to their loved ones, and became essential members of the workforce. While they were able to feel a certain amount of relief and satisfaction by taking an active part in the war effort, the men who could not go and fight for some reason found it embarrassing to be left at home.

Bertram Hutchings, the caravan-maker and food reformist, had been very distressed when he was refused for active service on health grounds. Like many businesses, his company had provided material support from the beginning of hostilities. His Winchester caravan hire fleet comprised fifteen caravans by 1914 and was complemented by a stable of twelve horses. The horses were commandeered at the same time that ponies and farm horses were collected from family paddocks and country fields all over Britain. Later the vans were taken for the use of detachments of the Red Cross and as quarters for officers. There was a great shortage of housing during the war for officers and men, and caravans were ideal for the purpose. The Red Cross already had some experience of vans, having been given two horse-drawn ones by a caravan enthusiast for the use of their nurses. These vans travelled to the Front but they never returned. In 1915, Bertram Hutchings was commissioned to build his first motor caravan. The Royal Navy needed a mobile recruiting office, and Mr Hutchings was enormously pleased to be able to use his expertise in designing an appropriate vehicle.

As the war progressed, the civilian taxis, buses and lorries that had been taken over by the Armed Forces in 1914 were replaced with more specialized equipment as the soldiers began to understand what kind of machinery they needed to fight a modern war. Purpose-built motor ambulances, staff cars, mobile surgeries and canteens, vans for wireless operators, trailers for photographers and travelling workshops appeared at the Front. Horses proved to be no match for the might of mechanical technology. They suffered shell shock like their riders and drivers; they succumbed to nerve gas; and they could not match the speed or the durability of motorized vehicles. They were used less and less, while the aeroplane, a machine seen as a fascinating oddity only a few years before, took on a crucial role. The Royal Flying Corps carried on a battle in the sky which, despite the appalling losses that it generated, captured the imagination of the British and filled them with great pride and determination. The pilots seemed to embody the spirit of defiant and modest courage that the country needed to carry on with the fight. A poet from the Royal Flying Corps wrote, in 1916:

Returning from my morning fly
I met a Fokker in the sky
And judging from its swift descent
It had a nasty accident.
On thinking further of the same
I rather fear I was to blame.[8]

An Overland motor caravan. Only the very well-to-do could afford to run a motor caravan in the 1920s – and pay the Chancellor of the Exchequer's newly introduced tax on horsepower.

The tone of his verse was exactly right for its purpose. The British civilians at that time were being bombed from the air by zeppelins. They needed all the poems and jokes that they could get to keep up their nerve. They no longer expected the war to be over quickly, nor did they know which side would eventually win. The arrival of the Americans in April of 1917 gave them new heart, but in the same month they were yet again asked to eat less bread, grow more of their own vegetables in allotments and to carry on digging for Britain while the Germans had the audacity to drop bombs on them in broad daylight, even in the middle of London. Ideas of pleasure had gone. A grim determination held the nation together. In April 1918, the Germans advanced again and the people read, with dread in their hearts, about the speech given by General Sir Douglas Haig to his men. He told them, 'With our backs to the wall, and believing in the justice of our cause, each one of us must fight to the end. The safety of our homes and the freedom of mankind depend alike upon the conduct of each one of us at the critical moment.'

Amid massive slaughter, the British held off the German attack. The French not only managed to hold their positions but to beat back the enemy. The British and Americans felt the impetus behind the Germans begin to slacken. They realized that it had been the last big effort left in the exhausted

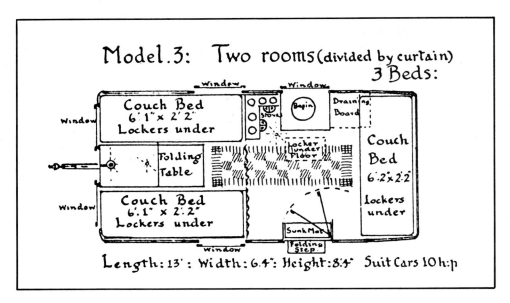

By the end of the 1920s, Major C. Fleming-Williams had turned his Car Cruiser company into a flourishing concern. He stocked his vans to include every possible utensil, down to the soap swish and the fish slice.

troops of the Kaiser, and they moved confidently forward. General Haig sent a message to the War Office as they advanced, calling for as many caravans as could be mustered for the use of his officers. He wanted his commanding officers to be able to live in their vans, keeping their maps and plans at hand day and night so that they could move quickly and efficiently with the attacking force. The War Office immediately got in touch with J. Harris Stone in his capacity as Secretary of the Caravan Club. Ordered to trace as many vans as he could in the next forty-eight hours, he telegraphed round the country. The Club meetings had dwindled almost to nothing during the war years but the members were still in contact, and about fifty caravans were made available. They were dusted off and dragged out of their stables and garages and back gardens to be shipped over to the continent.

In November the Armistice was signed. The young men and women who had survived came back to Britain. Within a year, four million men were released from the Armed Services. They came home to find dreadful weather, an influenza epidemic that killed off thousands of people at just the moment when they should have been confident of survival at the end of the war, and serious unemployment problems. People felt bad-tempered and fed up. Men returning from the Front could have hoped for a more cheerful homecoming, but they were a resilient group who had learned a great deal during their years at war, and many of them set about using the skills they had acquired in new enterprises.

All the vehicles that served the troops needed mechanics and drivers so there were plenty of men now trained in the maintenance of cars. Others had worked with aeroplanes, as pilots or as ground crew. They had acted on their own initiative in times of great stress, and they no longer wanted to go and work in dull jobs for peacetime bosses. In the trenches all classes of men mixed freely, and none of the soldiers who had known the feeling of an equal society wanted to return to the old subservient ways of master and men. With their discharge gratuities to use as capital, many of these ex-soldiers and airmen set up their own businesses. They started in a small way, often making use of the surplus war materials being sold off by the War Office now that the country was once more at peace.

One of these men was C. Fleming-Williams, who had spent the war in the Royal Flying Corps, and had been so besotted with the shape and design of aeroplanes that he was nicknamed 'Streamline Bill' by his colleagues in the services. After his discharge, he set up a company to make caravans, and soon designed a trailer van that was based on the same aerodynamic principle as an aeroplane wing. His interest in trailers began after he managed to move a grounded Bleriot monoplane during the war by dismounting its wings and dragging it along the road after his car. It towed behind him remarkably well, and started him thinking about the possible advantages of a caravan of similar construction. His first effort at a trailer van was dubbed by an unappreciative audience 'The Black Hole of Calcutta' since it had no back window and was designed to lower its resistance to the wind by narrowing at the top, so that the roof was smaller than the floor, and the user had the uncanny feeling that the walls were closing in on him.

Undaunted by the criticism, 'Streamline Bill' persevered with his company, Car Cruisers, and outlasted many of the other manufacturers who started out at the same time, many of whom in any case ended up by adopting several of his ideas. He was an enthusiastic and artistic man, who had worked as an illustrator before the War, and his advertisements reflected his romantic view of the world. Pretty girls, silhouetted against streamlined trailer caravans, gazed over lakes and moorland, or dawdled in grassy meadows. This image would have struck a chord with many people. For them the sky was a new and wonderful world to be explored, rather as the Nile had been a hundred years before. The plane, a miraculous and beautiful man-made bird, took twentieth-century heroes up into the clouds on their voyages of exploration. Those who yearned for the past and the good old pre-war days liked to see caravans that were shaped on the lines of the gypsy *vardos*, with bowed roofs and walls that sloped outwards. The caravanners who felt themselves to be part of the modern world wanted their vans to reflect the shape of the new romantic symbol, the aeroplane.

Miss Eva Hasell, the travelling missionary, could strip down the motor of her Ford motor caravan and put it back together with great proficiency.

144

Many strange versions of trailer were produced to be powered by motorbikes or bicycles, for buyers interested in the cheaper end of the market.

Another war veteran, Richard St Barbe Baker, belonged to the old school of caravanner by temperament. He loved trees with a passion, and had already started a degree in forestry at Cambridge when war broke out. When he was invalided out of the Army in April 1918 after being wounded for a second time, he returned to Cambridge to finish his course. Like many other undergraduates at that time he returned as a very mature student and needed more than the usual college activities to occupy his spare time. On an impulse, he bought ten railway truckloads of spare parts from H. M. Dispatch Board. He wanted to build himself a 'super-caravan' to satisfy his desire for a 'home on wheels in a sylvan setting'. While he continued to be fascinated by trees and the problems caused by the rapid erosion of woodland round the world, he also became very interested in trailer caravans during the next year. His prototype was built by the middle of 1919, and he then formed the Navarac Caravan Company.

The trucks from H. M. Dispatch Board had contained aeroplane under-carriages, plywood, spruce, canvas and various other bits and pieces useful for the construction of caravans. Baker hired several aircraftsmen with experience from the war days to help him, and began to build trailers for sale. He made enough to keep his workers employed and himself in pocket while he finished his degree. The trailers had lantern, or raised, roofs with windows let in along the sides to allow for light and ventilation, which gave them a quaint and old-fashioned appearance. They had four wheels and were fitted with a door at the front. They were equipped with a towing bar that was suitable for

The Flatavan chassis-and-trailer combination. Sleeping and dining 16 persons, it was built to the order of the Maharajah of Gwalior and was inspected by King George V and Queen Mary at Buckingham Palace before being shipped to India.

Women were always keen on caravanning. They found freedom in the unorthodox lifestyle that went with travelling and were ready to try out new ideas.

either a motor car or a horse, which meant that they were versatile in a world that was still split between tradition and technology.

It soon became clear that the motor would be the transport of the future and that two-wheeled trailers towed more successfully than those on four wheels, but before it became necessary to modify his designs, Richard St Barbe Baker was busy with other interests. He had always hoped to work in forestry and after he left Cambridge he applied to be the Assistant Conservator of Forests in Kenya. He was turned down on health grounds. Bitterly disappointed, he decided to go on a caravan tour to study the trees and forests of Europe. On the way to Southampton docks and the first phase of the journey, he paused in London to visit some of his old army friends. He was given permission to keep his caravan in the forecourt of Devonshire House, opposite Green Park, where he could look out of his window through the bars of the great iron gates and see the grass of the park beyond. The porter took messages from his friends at the gate and solemnly ushered them to the door when they came to visit. Having spent some time in what must be one of the most exclusive pitches ever used by a caravanner, he journeyed on to Southampton and was about to embark for Europe when he was summoned back for a further medical examination in relation to the post in Kenya. Having been pronounced fit, he sailed for Africa in 1920, following in the footsteps of his ancestor, Sir Samuel White Baker, who had travelled there almost a century before in order to explore the Nile.

Kenya was at that time turning rapidly into a desert because of the mass felling of trees. This indiscriminate destruction of the woodland was causing vast areas to dry up, and in an effort to make the native people aware of the importance of maintaining their forests, Baker hit upon the idea of composing a Dance of the Trees which was included at his request by the local chiefs in the ritual feast-day celebrations and met with great success. After the dancing Baker told the warriors that they were known throughout the world as 'Forest Destroyers'. The men were troubled by the idea, and responded eagerly to his suggestion that they band together and form a group called the Men of Trees. In order to belong to the society each man had to swear on oath that he would plant ten trees each year. Later the Boy Scout promise to do at least one good deed every day was added to the rules. If a member could find no other way to fulfil his daily act of kindness, then he could satisfy the requirement by planting another tree. The Men of Trees were all issued with a badge when they joined. Since the tribesmen did not wear many clothes, the badges could not be pinned, so they were made to be tied to the wrist by a leather strap decorated with white and green beads.

Young Kenyan warriors constituted the founder members of Men of Trees but they were soon joined by others from all over the world. Baker never returned to his trailer business, but instead spent his life travelling from country to country, preaching the doctrine of tree and soil renovation. Amongst his other achievements was the rescue of large numbers of redwood groves in Northern California that had been destined to fall under the lumberman's axe. He found the redwoods magnificent, and one grove in particular became a kind of Mecca for Men of Trees. The soaring trunks, which resembled the columns of a great cathedral, and the awesome quiet that prevailed in the twilight-coloured glades made the place a suitable shrine to the majesty of nature.

Richard St Barbe Baker did not invent the trailer caravan before he went off to Africa, any more than the other pioneer, C. Fleming-Williams; no one person could claim to have done so. Although versions appeared before the Great War, the first commercial vans were available from several sources, simultaneously, in 1919. They were often built as a sideline to developing car businesses. Soon there were many kinds, in all shapes and sizes. Some had two wheels and some had four. There were collapsible trailers and two-storeyed contraptions with tops that folded by day on to the bottom half and then cranked up at night to their full height. Most manufacturers were uncertain of the future for trailers and concentrated on motor caravans as their main concern. Some makers combined the two, by building cars that contained a compartment in the boot that could be pulled out at night to form a bed. The modification of this idea eventually culminated in the production of a car that included the most extraordinary collection of folding objects in the history of the caravan. Not only did the bed fold into the boot of the car, but there was a folding table and two stools which fitted in the back of the driver's seat. There was also a collapsible fabric washstand, and an arrangement in the boot which allowed it to swing up on hinges to reveal a complete portable toilet set.

In 1920, the Chancellor of the Exchequer put a tax on cars by imposing a levy of £1 per unit of horsepower. The motor caravan and trailer business suffered badly from this law. Although the public continued to drive cars in increasing numbers, they considered a motor caravan, which was heavy and needed a powerful engine, or a trailer that required a strong car to tow it easily, to be a luxury they could not afford. The trade in pleasure vans suffered a long hiccup, and the Caravan Club dwindled in its activities until it became nothing more than a yearly excuse for dinner dances for life members. Apart from the caravans used by showmen and gypsies, most vans belonged to very keen enthusiasts indeed, or to the eccentric and rich few who were unaffected by the imposition of the tax. Many of the wealthy clients went to Melville Hart, A.M.I.N.A., a designer who had his offices in Westminster and specialized in one-off caravans that were built to the specification of the buyer. They ranged from two-wheeled trailers to four-wheeled, 20-foot-long vans, equipped with every luxury and drawn by big pneumatic-tyred motor tractors. They were often sold to eminent foreign buyers and some of them were taken, before they were shipped off, to be viewed at Buckingham Palace or the Houses of Parliament.

If you could afford the tax on horsepower, another 5 shillings would buy anyone a licence. There was no need to show proficiency at the wheel. In 1922 there were a million cars on the road, and it must be assumed that a large number of people travelling were driving themselves rather than relying on the skills of a chauffeur. It became customary to see women at the wheel of a car during the Great War, when they took jobs as drivers for Army officers and for the Red Cross. After the war, they continued to enjoy motoring, and some, like Eva Hasell, moved from driving motor cars to motor caravans during the 1920s. She was born, in 1886, into a rich and religious family who lived in a manor house in Cumberland which had been occupied by the Hasell family since the seventeenth century. In 1914 she enrolled at St Christopher's College in Blackheath in order to train as a Sunday-school organizer, but when the war interrupted her course, she went to drive an ambulance for the Red Cross. At the end of the war, Miss Hasell returned to her studies, and then began to work with Sunday-school teachers in her local area. However, she had a great desire for challenge and adventure, and when two colleagues from her days at St Christopher's sent a letter suggesting that she join them in western Canada to teach Sunday school, she accepted with alacrity. Canada was a largely uncultivated and sparsely populated area in the 1920s. Settlers sometimes saw no one outside their own family for months at a time. Church districts were huge. One clergyman on horseback would have charge of four thousand miles of territory, and because so many clergy were killed in the war it was hard to supply enough men to provide even this scanty service. The Sunday-school teachers had real problems in finding ways to reach large numbers of children, and they considered many different ideas before they decided to try to find a horse-drawn caravan which could be equipped with living quarters and a bookstall, to be taken round the prairies by a teacher. When they contacted Eva Hasell, it was with the proposal that she should come out and travel in such a caravan. She agreed with the proposition, but with one alteration. She insisted on using a motor van. She explained that she was a good driver, because of her war experience, and that she knew a bit about engines, both from her training with the ambulance and because she had taken to servicing the family car at home after the chauffeur was called up.

She was very excited at the prospect of her adventure, and ordered a van to be made in Canada to her specifications ready for her arrival. She set off in February 1920, accompanied by a fellow worker, on a boat out of Liverpool. Although her colleague was horribly sick for a week, Eva Hasell loved the voyage, and was an object of amazement to the waiters because she ate

This Flatavan ('super caravan') accommodated three persons, with fitted saloon, kitchen, bathroom, a hot and cold water system and electric light. Melville Hart designed lavish caravans for the very rich, to their own specifications.

absolutely everything that they put in front of her. She enjoyed food enormously, never controlled her appetite, and consequently grew from a short, stocky young woman into a solid old woman. She was not in the least bothered about her weight, and cheerfully related a story about a parishioner in Canada who concluded that her partner did all the work because she was skinny and that Miss Hasell must be very lazy to have become so fat. In fact, she worked tirelessly. While she waited for the van to be completed on her arrival in Canada, she enrolled in a motor school to have a course of lessons on driving a Ford and in the repair and maintenance of its engine. By the time she set off in her van, which was mounted on a Ford chassis and fitted with an electric starter and lights, she could strip down an engine if necessary and put it all back together with great proficiency.

She found it hard to drive her caravan at first, because it was long and heavy and difficult to control on roads that were worse than the poorest cart-tracks to be found in England at that time. After travelling all day at a maximum speed of 10 miles an hour, she and her companion camped near to farmhouses by night so that they could obtain water. They had great difficulty undressing in the back of the van because Miss Hasell was too hefty to turn around properly in the narrow space left once the mattresses were lowered from their fixings on the walls. They took to pitching a tent beside the van to use as a dressing-room. Their mirrors were soon smashed by the jolting of the rutted roads, but the women were unworried by their appearance. They tidied their hair by regarding their shadows cast upon the ground, or by peering at the windscreen of the van. Their clothes were chosen strictly for utilitarian purposes and were expected to withstand mud and rain and dirt. Wherever they went the women landed in puddles, stuck in bogs and stalled in dust storms. Local farmers unfailingly dug them out and dusted them off. People who had almost nothing to spare offered hospitality in isolated towns with names like Moose Jaw, Eyebrow and Elbow. In Riverhurst, much to Miss Hasell's delight, they found a good Chinese restaurant where they had an excellent three-course meal for 1s 8d. While they were eating, the local policeman arrived to question them closely about their movements. The two women were dressed in khaki-coloured blouses, skirts and jackets, rubber boots and felt hats, a uniform that led to their nickname, amongst the children of western Canada, of 'Brownies'. It is likely that their faces were badly swollen from mosquito bites, since these were a common nuisance. Their van had been dubbed 'that grey booze-van' by many people who lived near to the American border, where a good deal of bootlegging took place. When they travelled along the border and crossed over it to reach one part of their district, the local bishop accompanied them for fear that they would be embarrassed by officers searching for contraband liquor. He need not have worried. Eva Hasell was perfectly capable of dealing with any situation that arose. She enjoyed being questioned by the policeman in Riverhurst. Crises put her on her mettle, and she was at her best when she took the lead, ready to sort out problems by her own methods. She was a powerful personality who liked her own way; tireless in pursuit of her goals but difficult to handle if crossed.

She had a series of fellow-workers for the first few summers that she spent establishing Sunday schools around Canada. She used a newly built van, in a different district, each summer, then, having set up Sunday-school classes in the remote townships, she donated the caravan she had travelled in to the local diocese on the understanding that it would be used to continue the work that she had started. In 1926, she took along a woman called Iris Sayle as her co-worker, and from then on the two women went together every year, having established such a strong relationship that they also shared a home in Britain in the wintertime. Iris Sayle was a perfect partner. She did not take the initiative away from Eva Hasell, or question her authority, and she dutifully clothed her large and angular frame in the Brownie uniform. Her only known foible was a liking for hats.[9]

By 1928 nine vans were operating in Canada, and Eva Hasell was financially responsible for them all. She ruled the mission with an iron hand, resisted all attempts by the Joint Van Committee that had been formed to allow men to crew the caravans, and insisted on using a majority of well-bred British girls for the job. She toured boarding schools in the winter and whipped up interest amongst the girls in order to provide future recruits. If they applied to spend a summer in Canada they could expect no salary, and many volunteers paid their own passage. They had to submit two references, one of which was to be from their local clergyman. He would be sent a questionnaire which included such questions as 'Do you think she would act with discretion among young unmarried men?' and 'Is she good-tempered and easy to get on with under difficult circumstances?'

As the years passed, Eva Hasell held control over the missionary vans against increasing opposition from the Canadian Church. Since this Church was well established by the mid-twentieth century, it considered it appropriate for Canadians to assume responsibility for the vans. There were many squabbles, and Miss Hasell more than once used the threat of withdrawing her substantial funds in order to maintain her position of authority. She finally relinquished control shortly before her death in 1974. Although they must by then have been relieved to be free from her domination and autocratic ways, the Canadian Church authorities were well aware of her stalwart qualities. Stubborn and determined, outspoken in her political views (which were violently anti-Communist), she set out in 1920 to care for the bodies and souls of the children of Canada, then dedicated the rest of her life and a considerable amount of her financial resources to the pursuit of her

Mr Kingsley Auster's Shadow caravan (a) raised, (b) lowered. Folding trailers were popular in the 1920s, but they could prove awkward when they stuck open in damp weather.

objective. She was an efficient fund-raiser, and was greatly admired by many people, including the Queen Mother, who visited one of her vans in the company of King George VI and always gave generously to the various van appeals. In 1935 she was awarded the MBE, but throughout their long career together Iris Sayle received no honour. She stayed in Eva Hasell's shadow, a faithful follower, until her death in 1973. Eva Hasell missed her terribly, and spent her days wandering sadly from room to room of the house that they had shared together for so many years, looking hopelessly for her friend and calling out her name.

CHAPTER 12

TWENTIETH-CENTURY TRAVELLERS

The highly ornate horse-drawn gypsy *vardos* never recovered their popularity after the First World War, even among nomadic travellers. Many showmen had already made the change to steam-transported wagons in any case, and after 1918 those who had stayed with the horses moved rapidly on to the use of trailers that could be pulled by motor cars or linked together in a chain to be taken by lorry to the next pitch. The only horses that still travelled with the shows were those used by performers in the ring. The circus-tent shows toured during the summer months, when the warmer weather made it possible to erect a big top on the 'tober' (piece of ground selected for the circus site) without danger of its being washed away in the winter rains or deterring customers who did not want to freeze to death while they watched the show. In the winter the circus acts performed in theatres or pantomimes. In earlier times they would have been housed in the traditional permanent circus buildings that flourished in the centres of big cities. The first of these was erected by Philip Astley, a retired cavalry instructor who had failed to earn a living as a riding master, and set himself up instead in 1770 as an equine exhibitor in an attempt to support himself. He eventually built an amphitheatre in Westminster Bridge Road in London – with money, it was rumoured, that he obtained through the sale of an unclaimed diamond ring found after one of his exhibition performances. The new hall was an immediate success, and other proprietors started their own circuses. When the circus boom was at its height some owners had several shows on the go at the same time. The large halls and hippodromes that were built to hold the circuses were also used for meetings and agricultural shows, and were later adapted to accommodate ice rinks and motor-car displays. As well as giving winter performances in the amphitheatres, the circus proprietors decided to send their shows on the road for the summer months, and many battles were fought in country lanes between rival groups of circus performers, when one proprietor would try to cut into a route that his rival considered to be his own private territory.

The people who worked in the circuses formed a very tight-knit commun-

Whether the trucks and vans were steam-driven, horse-drawn or equipped with motor engines, they never failed to sink into any mud around and would have to be manhandled out of trouble.

ity. The various acts were often family affairs, with the skills involved being passed on from mother to daughter or father to son. Children grew up watching their parents performing and practising every day, and they learned to balance on a tightrope, throw knives or ride bareback on the circus ponies almost before they could walk. The families lived in each other's pockets, in vans that were often sumptuously furnished but which were still too cramped to allow space for badly behaved children. Their profession encouraged them to lead disciplined and orderly lives, and parents who spent their time perfecting new acts and maintaining the excellence of the tricks that they had learned from their own parents brought up their families within a strict framework of cleanliness and obedience. Since they usually mixed with their own kind almost exclusively, the daughters of famous circus families frequently married the sons of others. They would often develop an act together: the wife might, for example, stand against a board in the ring while her husband threw knives around the outline of her body; having done that, she would go back to the wagon to get his supper ready. The degree of trust and intimacy needed for a relationship of that kind formed very strong and lasting bonds

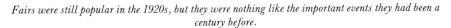

Fairs were still popular in the 1920s, but they were nothing like the important events they had been a century before.

Early circuses, in amphitheatres built specially for the purpose, drew large crowds from all classes.
Charles Dickens was a great enthusiast.

between the couples. When the children were also involved in the act, and entrusted their lives to the rest of their family night after night, it became unthinkable that the various members might split up over anything but the most violent of disagreements.

Despite the very respectable lives of its performers, the circus had a bad reputation. There was always some apprehension in towns and villages at the news that the circus was coming. Those circus members who did not have their own living wagons found it difficult to find lodgings. Suspicious landladies would put up a 'No Vacancies' sign if they thought there was likely to be a circus performer on their doorstep. Housewives hurried to take in their washing for fear that it would be pinched. They had reason to worry. Joe the Clown, a member of the Great Carmo's Circus, had a story about a time when the circus with which he was travelling one summer passed along a country lane in the dead of night. Somebody spotted something white gleaming in the moonlight above the hedgerow. He looked closer, and saw that a cottager had left her washing out on the line at the edge of her garden. He passed the word to the others, and they quickly grabbed all the clothes that were hanging there and exchanged them for the dirty shirts they were wearing. For the next few days the tent men went about their business dressed in women's chemises and lace-edged drawers.

Trouble at the circus did not always start because of the visiting performers. The suspicion of the townspeople occasionally led to bad behaviour on the part of local troublemakers. They came looking for a fight, or hoping to set fire to the tents and wagons. Joe the Clown told another story about a night when the circus was attacked during an evening performance. One of the tent hands suddenly noticed that a hole had been cut in the canvas of the big top and that a man's face was peering through. The tent hand was furious, and gave the intruding face a shove. A scuffle ensued, attracting the attention of other villagers, who joined in and started throwing stones at the circus workers, who were meanwhile struggling to get down the big top before it suffered any more damage. The crowd managed to push three of the wagons into a nearby river before it was finally dispersed, which was not until the women of the circus had grabbed the shooting-gallery guns and fired them into the air. When dawn broke, the extent of the destruction and injury to workers became apparent. Several of the tent hands were suffering from split heads; however, no one was very concerned about them, because they never appeared in front of the paying public and did not need to look attractive. The only real problem was a spectacular broken nose that marred the beauty of the jockey rider's face beyond all hope of immediate repair.[10]

Guns were used more than once to protect the circus. A mob could easily be put into an ugly mood by the exciting atmosphere that a circus generated. It was a place where civilization met the jungle, and man barely controlled the savage power of the beast. In Great Carmo's Circus, the lion-tamer Togare moved nightly amongst his charges, half naked himself, his body glistening under the lights of the big top. Lady Eleanor Smith, an author and one of his greatest admirers, dubbed him the 'Valentino of the Ring'. For his fascinated audience, there was an element of primeval attraction to danger as they watched him in action. The balance between destruction and domination was held by the mesmeric power of his personality as he cajoled and bullied his lions through their act.

Togare was in fact devoted to his animals. Half Turk and half Serb, he was born into a peasant family and apprenticed as a boy to a butcher. He ran away, living on the fringes of the travelling fairgrounds and surviving as a boxer in the booths. After a few years he met Lola Pietro, a Mexican who worked with a troupe of fifteen polar bears. He started to help her to train the bears, and then he married her. His skill at working with animals led him to take on the big cats, and he discovered that he had a great gift for handling them. His affection for the animals was returned in full measure. The artist Dame Laura Knight, who knew Togare well, was at the circus to witness an

After the demise of the Great Carmo's Circus, Dame Laura Knight turned her attention to the gypsies, and painted their vans and camp-sites with the same enthusiasm that she had shown in the past for the circus and its performers.

extraordinary scene. One of the lions, Paris, got a bone shard caught in his gum. Togare found some pliers and tried time and again to wrench the bone from the lion's mouth. At one point, he caused him such pain that Paris's eyes narrowed, his body tensed, and he was transformed before the horrified eyes of all those watching him into a savage killer. As he moved to strike, he saw through his fury that the man in front of him was Togare. His expression softened, his muscles relaxed, and he allowed his trainer to force open his jaws once more and successfully remove the piece of bone. When he was later sold to the Berlin Zoo, Togare was swollen-eyed with grief when the time came for his lion to go to Germany, and Paris pined away for love of his old trainer.

Animal trainers were highly paid and glamorous people. They attracted followers and met many interesting people. The circus had always drawn a proportion of wealthy and respectable admirers who were fascinated by the raw excitement as well as by the defiance of the laws of nature. Dame Laura Knight found the atmosphere so compelling that she spent night after night watching the performers. She had always been interested in people who trained their bodies to high peaks of excellence. She drew pictures of boxers, acrobats and dancers, either at their work or waiting to go on stage in the wings or in their dressing-rooms. She spent many years backstage at the ballet before she was introduced to the circus by friends. She then met the show proprietor, Sir Bertram Mills, through her friend Sir Alfred Munnings, and embarked upon a long series of pictures drawn first from the performances at the Agriculture Hall and Olympia in London, and then from the scenes she saw when she travelled with the great Carmo's Circus in the summer of 1931. She shared digs with Joe the Clown and his wife Ally and kept all her canvases and paints in one of Mr Carmo's vans. Her obsession with the show was so strong that her husband, Sir Harold Knight, called her 'circus-crazy'. She was often away for months at a time, painting and drawing and living with the entertainers.

Many gypsies turned from horse-dealing to scrap-metal trading, but there was still some business left in the sale of ponies. Either way, the gypsy could make a living and keep on the move at the same time.

Although trailers became more and more common after the First World War, some travellers retained their traditional caravans. Even if they used a car for travelling, gypsies usually kept some horses around as well for sentimental reasons.

In the 'thirties, the public grew tired of horses and cars on the merry-go-round and preferred to sit astride exotic birds or animals.

Many gypsy vans were fitted with stoves, but it was still considered preferable to cook out of doors.

The Depression had begun to take its toll on box-office receipts, and the Great Carmo decided to risk taking the circus on the road in the winter to make some extra money. The tour was a disaster. He was forced to sell up, splitting his animals between various zoos and rival circuses and disbanding his team of performers. Dame Laura Knight was particularly sad when he sold his train of three living wagons to a rich man who wanted them in order that he might spend a few days of his leisured life on the road each year. Although her interest in the circus remained, and her friendship with many of the performers continued, Dame Laura Knight never travelled with any other circus after the collapse of the Great Carmo's show.

Lady Eleanor Smith, who had been accompanying Mr Carmo's circus in the same summer of 1931, used some of his performers as the basis for a best-selling novel that she wrote while she travelled. She was attracted to the circus for much the same reasons as Dame Laura Knight. The daughter of Lord Birkenhead, the Lord Chancellor, she grew up in a world of wealth and privilege, but she had very little interest in débutante balls and society dinners. She loved horses and riding, even as a small child, so when she grew up she was keen to join in any activity that involved them. After reading *Lavengro* at the age of nine, she developed the fantasy that her father had gypsy blood inherited from his grandmother and continued to claim a connection with the gypsies all her life. Since horses are the lifeblood of a circus, she was naturally drawn to the big top. While Dame Laura Knight sat at the back, painting the performers in their dressing-rooms, Lady Eleanor Smith sat in the front, drinking in the excitement and danger, then distilling her feelings into material for her book. The *Red Wagon* cheated slightly – by introducing a gypsy element into a circus story when in reality the two worlds had little to do with each other – but it made a compelling story. Even Winston Churchill read the book and complimented Lady Eleanor's father on the skill with which it had been written. Lord Birkenhead, who had always been rather sceptical of his daughter's talents, was so pleased that he bought her a brooch shaped like a caravan, with the wagon body made out of rubies and the wheel spokes and window of diamonds.

In real life gypsies were rarely found near the circus. They spent more time in the fairgrounds telling fortunes or running sideshows. There was still, even after the First World War, a reasonable trade in horses in country areas, and the traditional fairs were well attended by gypsies, who were most reluctant to give up their favourite meeting places. Silvester Boswell, who had worked with his gypsy parents in a mission tent at the turn of the century, was still engaged in horse-dealing during the 1920s. After an adolescence spent helping out at fairgrounds and pulling bathing machines down the beaches at seaside resorts during the summer seasons, he found himself in the Veterinary Corps during the war. He was responsible for the care of horses that had

Barnet Fair, 1919. Gypsy families tended to be large and scattered. Members stayed in touch with each other by attending the traditional fairs held round the country at set dates during the year.

suffered from shell shock and were wasting away despite all efforts to save them. After his discharge he returned to his old haunts at Whitby, Halifax and Huddersfield. Although the number of customers was dwindling all the time there were still some lucrative outlets. The Italian ice-cream sellers in Leeds used ponies for their carts, and some farmers still preferred to work with horses, although tractors were becoming more common everywhere. Even the gypsy families started to buy trailers and cars, although they always kept a few horses around as well because of the strong sentimental attachment they felt for them.

Silvester Boswell himself bought a trailer in 1927 and started to move out of horse-trading and into scrap-metal dealing. This was a popular occupation for a lot of gypsies. It kept them on the move, slightly outside normal society, and it proved, despite the odd bad year, to be a profitable business. Some gypsies carried on living in their trailers all the year round. Others, like Boswell, eventually bought houses. When Silvester invited his old father to come and live with him, the invitation was accepted, but the old man kept his van and slept in it at night as he had always done. Other gypsies found it harder and harder to wander the countryside at will because local councils began to feel bound to introduce special sites in the interests of hygiene. The numbers of people in caravans had begun to increase by the end of the 'twenties, when not only the gypsies but people down on their luck began to occupy semi-permanent sites by the roadsides, and holiday-makers from the cities, and particularly from the Midlands, started to fill the fields beside the seaside at weekends and during the summer holidays. Some sort of control was badly needed if the caravan, which had once been a symbol of extravagance, was to salvage its increasingly bad reputation with the public.

CHAPTER 13

THE GOLDEN YEARS

The main problem for those who wanted to maintain the good image of the caravan was the sudden and dramatic rise in popularity that trailers experienced at the end of the 1920s and especially in the 1930s. This change of fortune was directly linked to the new movement towards compulsory holidays that developed during the first three decades of the twentieth century. By 1900 members of the middle class expected to take an annual holiday away from home and the better-paid manual workers were beginning to demand the same. Travel agents such as Thomas Cook made the problems of foreign travel much less alarming, since their agents were able to take care of difficulties arising from language barriers, exchange rates and bureaucratic muddles over passports and visas. For those who wanted to remain within the British Isles, there were tours organized by travel agents or camps, most of which had sprung up since the First World War, at various scenic spots. These catered for motorists, cyclists, caravanners and pedestrians by offering them self-contained settlements where, for an all-in charge, they could have all their needs cared for. Because these sites developed without any outside authority or organization to oversee them, their quality varied considerably; some sites were very shabby indeed.

As the years passed, more and more people were looking for places to go for their holidays. The idea of holidays as a right, something that the TUC included rather half-heartedly in a resolution as early as 1911, really began to take hold in the 1920s. Reluctant employers realized that they were going to have to go along with the modern trend and allow their workers at least a week off each year. By 1928 the papers were full of holiday hints, particularly for the ladies. There were articles on vacation outfits, beauty tips for make-up out of doors, hints on staying cool in hot weather and recipes for using up the milk that had gone sour in the caravan larder overnight. In July, a heatwave baked the families crowded on to the beaches and a series of bathing tragedies were reported in the press. Motor correspondents wrote warning stories about the possible dire consequences to be suffered by drivers who neglected their tyres in hot weather; the writer Storm Jameson did a piece on the advantages to be found in separate holidays for husbands and wives; and the American author Sinclair Lewis wrote a series of articles about his experiences while travelling in a motor caravan. The interest in caravan holidays was now firmly established, and the enthusiasm was further fanned by the *Daily Express* correspondent for motoring when he wrote about his tour in his Car Cruiser trailer, called 'Hedgerow Villa', in 1931.

People had seen trailers before. In the early days of commercial caravan companies, dealers spent a good deal of their time cruising round busy streets in the hope of publicizing their products. Collapsible trailers, particularly a model called the Shadow, introduced in 1925, had been reasonably successful, and anyone who spent the summer around Aberdovey in Wales after 1921 would probably have seen some of the rather bizarre trailers from a fleet of motorbike-drawn caravans that were hired out by a well-known figure from the biking world, A.G. Cocks. The original reluctance by the public to buy a caravan, because of the expense, became less of a difficulty during the 1920s as their incomes steadily rose in real terms; by the end of the decade a great many people were driving their own 7-horsepower cars, the favourite makes

The Winchester 14–foot 6–inch two-compartment trailer caravan de luxe. The Winchester caravan was one of the first truly popular trailers. It was designed by Bertram Hutchings, who had an uncanny feeling for the market trends of the moment.

Stylish young couples took to trailer holidays once the vans became fashionable and reasonably priced.

A dog was still considered an important member of the party in the 1930s.

being Jowetts and Austins. Bertram Hutchings, always good at interpreting the mood of his public, designed a trailer seven-and-a-half feet long with a plain roof which he called the Tom Thumb. It was exactly the right, light, easily manoeuvrable sort of van to use with the cars currently on the road, and it cost £87. This was a lot more than anyone would have to spend on a small folding trailer, but it was far more convenient and it sold well. He followed it with a deluxe version, called Lady Nimble, which featured a lantern roof, cavity walls for better insulation, and an emergency toilet, a proprietary closet called a Vantour, one of a growing number of contraptions introduced in an attempt to deal with the very difficult problem of sanitary arrangements on tour.

It was chiefly because of these problems that more and more people pressed for legislation to be brought in to deal with caravan camps. When the first-ever magazine to deal exclusively with caravans was published in May 1933, its pages were full of reports on the possible restrictions planned by impending government moves against the traveller. When the magazine published its first issue, with the sub-title 'The only magazine for those who love the gypsy life', 3,500 caravans were in use in Britain. Many of their users had gathered the summer before at the first trailer rally, organized by the magazine *Autocar*. The RAC held another in 1933, and the presentation of prizes at these events for the best-designed vans of the year started a spurt of competition between the various rival trailer companies. Debate over the relative advantages of lantern roofs over plain ones, inward- or outward-sloping walls, the lack of headroom in streamlined models and the most useful types of tow-bar led to a surge of interest by designers, who produced innovative features ready for the yearly competitions, and guarded their ideas jealously until they were unveiled for the judges and the ever-increasing crowds of admiring spectators at caravan events.

These crowds were made up of ordinary men and women who had little interest in a bohemian existence. *Caravan and Trailer* soon dropped its sub-title referring to gypsy life, perhaps because the public image of the gypsy was reverting to the old notion of a shifty traveller who would leave rubbish behind him and clutter up the view with his ugly van.

As the numbers of caravanners increased, the hostility of the general public grew in proportion. Motorists loathed trailers. In 1930, the Road Traffic Act abolished the universal 20-mph speed limit. In the new allocations of maximum speeds, cars with two-wheeled pneumatic-tyred trailers were permitted to travel up to 30 miles per hour. Motorists, keen to enjoy the pleasure of their own less restricted speed, were furious to find themselves stuck behind the much slower trailers on the holiday routes to the coasts or to the Lake District. There were no motorways. Passing a trailer could take a long time. The driver of the car pulling the trailer was probably a family man taking his wife and children on a cheap holiday, and perhaps pulling a hired caravan for the first time in his life. He would find it quite difficult to control his trailer, particularly if the wind were strong. He caused a very real annoyance and sometimes represented a hazard to the impatient motorist behind him. The clamour for legislation grew.

It was hard for the authorities to know how to deal with the dilemma. People on holiday for a week or two from the big cities liked to find themselves amongst crowds. Amusement parks, seaside concerts and theatres flourished because they were full, and the jolly atmosphere drew more and more people to them. A weekly holiday by the sea cost about £10 by the end of the 1930s for a man with his wife and two children, assuming they stayed in rented accommodation. The majority of working men were earning £4 a week or less, and the cost was too high for them. However, they still wanted to go away. They had seen all the photos in the paper of titled children playing in the sand and read about the best way to keep sandwiches fresh in the midday sun, and they wanted to join in and have a good time like everyone else. In a country where advertising was in full swing, and the population was urged to spend money on one new fad after another, the people were indignant if they were excluded from the entertainment that they had come to see as their right. The answer to the problem seemed to be holiday camps. Several of these were formed by worthy organizations such as the Co-operative Wholesale Society and Workers Travel Association, who first opened a camp in 1939 as a non-profit-making venture. Local boroughs contemplated setting up camps of their own.

Far more popular, however, were the Butlins camps, where there was more excitement on offer to the paying customer. For an all-in price, a reasonable sum of money, the holidaymaker was given room and board, free tuition in sports, a child-minding service, nightly entertainment and organized competitions. This was a much more attractive proposition than places that seemed dangerously close to being charity organizations. When a luxury Butlins camp opened in Skegness in 1936 it was packed out. It was followed by another at Clacton. Newspapers began to predict confidently that there would be hundreds of such camps within the foreseeable future, and that they would be able to satisfy all the holiday needs of the man in the street. The less regimented variety of camps that had sprung up in anarchical fashion around the resorts over the years was restricted by legislation passed at various intervals during the 1930s, but they managed to survive in any case. The numbers of people wanting to go away, especially in the peak weeks in July and August, were so great that there was nowhere else to accommodate them.

Pleasure coaches carried 82 million passengers in 1936–7. These people mostly had two weeks in which to enjoy themselves, and very little spare cash with which to finance their enjoyment. Many continued to cram into badly

Mr Presland, of the London Caravan Club, arriving at the Rally held on 12 May 1935 at Wickstead Park, Kettering. Once revived, the Club went from strength to strength.

organized shanty sites by the sea. Others took advantage of the camping coaches set up by the four mainline railway companies. These were carriages that had been converted into caravans and left in sidings, by the sea or in the countryside. They were quite successful with the public, and by 1939 there were over four hundred of them scattered about the outer reaches of the railway network.

A lot of young people camped. The Camping Club of Great Britain estimated that half a million people took their holidays in tents during 1938. These campers were often sharing sites with caravanners who joined the caravan section of the Camping Club that had been started in 1921. In 1935, the Honorary Secretary of the caravan section, Major K. Vernon C. Brook, was driven by exasperation to write an open letter to the *Caravan and Trailer* magazine criticizing the seaside sites which he found 'almost insanitary and indecent'. He blamed the overcrowding and rowdy conditions mostly on young campers. Caravanners, he claimed, were more fastidious over sanitation and usually not addicted to constant mechanical music. He hastened to assure his readers that his views had nothing to do with snobbism, but he felt that caravanners were different by temperament from the average camper

Packed to the rafters with children, buckets and spades and suitcases, trailers became a menace to other motorists on the road to the coast.

and that they would be much happier if there were a way to arrange for them to holiday in greater seclusion. His recommendation was that several sites, possibly half a dozen on each of the three coasts of Great Britain, could be reserved exclusively for the use of caravanners; they would pay a subscription for the use of the site and for the services of an orderly farmer or landlord, who would be expected to empty rubbish bins daily, deliver letters and carry round the milk. He felt that at an extra cost to caravanners of perhaps 10–15 shillings a year, there would be a great many people ready to go along with his idea. The editor of *Caravan and Trailer* commented at the bottom of the published letter that this arrangement would only work if there were approved caravans on such sites, since there were presently some shacks-on-wheels claiming to be caravans which would lower the tone of any place in which they were parked.

While caravan-users and commentators were sorting out the difficulties at sites in Britain and gradually working their way towards the formation of sites of the type that we know today, many holidaymakers were venturing abroad with their caravans. They may have been inspired by articles written by caravan dealers who had taken new trailer models on endurance tests in order to boost the publicity and encourage sales. The opening issue of *Caravan and Trailer* featured a story about the dealer Dudley H. Noble, who set off from London for Cairo early in 1933. His trailer was piled high with the baggage for a crew of five, water tanks and a dozen tins of petrol, and it literally weighed a ton. At first, the journey went well and the party sped along at 40 miles an hour on tarred roads. Then the roads diminished into tracks, and the car travelled most of the rest of the way in low gear. The expedition was slowed further when the trailer collided at night with a camel-drawn cart. This rather symbolic accident, involving a modern caravan with one of the essential ingredients of a caravan in the ancient meaning of the word, resulted in the trailer being dented but usable and the camel unaffected. When Cairo finally came in view, Dudley Noble had covered 3000 miles in 21 days. He was very pleased with his progress, and was full of praise for his Hillman Wizard car, which had done 12½ miles to the gallon and generally lived up to its name.

Another expedition, headed by Clive Scarff, the managing director of Nomad Caravan Company, toured the Sahara in a Humber Snipe, towing an Eccles Nymphette three-berth trailer. They travelled 660 miles across France to Marseilles, then two thousand miles around North Africa before returning to Britain via Marseilles again. The trip started on 28 November 1934 and returned less than a month later on 22 December. The only purpose of trips of this nature was to prove the durability of the vehicles involved, although they also showed that the crews were pretty tough. No mention was made of pleasure taken in the scenery or amusing incidents along the way.

The need for an ability to endure whilst engaged in foreign travel was eloquently voiced in a letter from the private traveller Herbert Shultz, who set off with his wife and three children in a family car towing a Rice Long Standard caravan in October of 1933 and eventually arrived at his destination in Bombay in May 1934. He warned that although the tour was perfectly pleasant until Turin, he thereafter learned that it was foolhardy to attempt to cross overland to India in any months other than June, July and August. The hardships that he and his family suffered while travelling during the winter months were greater than the adventure justified. He wrote of unmade roads, rivers with no bridges, huge stretches of marshland, and of an 850-mile dash across the last leg of the journey from Madras to Bombay when the end of their ordeal came in sight. Having announced, 'I should never for one moment consider a second trip like this,' he saved what praise he had to offer for his foldaway trailer, which had performed excellently throughout the trip under appalling conditions.

Other travellers sent long accounts to the *Caravan and Trailer* about their exploits in deserts around the world. They were usually accompanied by tiny, indistinct photographs, like those contributed by Major Huddle after his successful crossing of the Sahara Desert en route to Kenya. Most of these pictures appeared to have been taken into the sun by a photographer who is trying to get as much sky as possible into the frame and to use Egyptian tombs or men in safari suits as scale models for the vast cloud formations that tower above them. Dorothy Una Ratcliffe was so delighted with her experiences while travelling that she wrote a book about it all, called *South African Summer: 5000 Miles with a Car and Caravan Trailer*. Her trailer for the trip was made in Winchester by Bertram Hutchings. When she arrived at his yard to collect it, she found it sandwiched between a grey van with 'Prepare Ye the Way of the Lord' painted on the side and a much gayer *vardo* made for a group of hop-picking gypsies. However bright this van might have been, it could hardly have competed with Mrs Ratcliffe's caravan. This 15-foot-long Winchester model had been painted, at her request, crocus yellow above and brown below with a marigold belt to separate the colours. Mrs Ratcliffe described the effect when seen from a distance as 'like a large dis-winged bumble-bee'. She was thrilled with it, and with the yard from which it came. She gazed kindly on Jack, the carpenter at Hutchings, who had actually made her van. To her romantic eyes he seemed 'a Hardy figure'. She described in her book 'his chiselled features, finely-lined skin, slight stoop and masterly hands, his clean apron and everything about him denoting a love of timber and good tools'. If Jack's hands were masterly and his features chiselled, they still did not match those of her husband and fellow companion on the South African trip, the Laird. He was 'strong, well-knit, sunburnt and wind-roughened, with finely-shaped hands a trifle neglected. Good-tempered

Trailers were becoming popular by 1934, and were often hired by families who wanted a cheap holiday.

In 1931 it was still possible to find a deserted riverbank and set up camp in idyllic seclusion, although these bathing beauties look as though they would have preferred a crowded site in a holiday resort.

looking, but tough and obstinate.' He might have stepped out of the pages of any romantic novel. His character, so clearly defined at the start of the book, remained consistent throughout the account of the adventure. His obstinacy was particularly noticeable, and it provided a perfect foil for the equally constant portrayal of the author as a woman of sweet understanding and charming temperament. Having spent many happy hours making lists together of the necessary provisions for the journey in the 'African Marigold', the couple discovered in Cape Town that they had stupidly forgotten to pack a mustard pot. They put off the start of their trek until they managed to find just the one that the Laird wanted, and wrapped it carefully to take its place amongst the other essential items for the trip. Pre-eminent amongst these was the teapot, which was vital since the Laird was unable to contemplate life without a decent cup of tea. His first cup of the day was brought to him as the early-morning sun streamed in through the marigold curtains, which covered the diamond panes of the caravan windows, by one Hal Green, who came along on the trip to do the cooking. Unlike the other characters in this book, he remained a shadowy figure, mentioned only at times when the caravan needed to be dragged out of flooded rivers or when ants invaded the meatsafe.

The ants were not the only creatures that broke into the caravan. Mrs Ratcliffe found a pretty brown donkey one day in the act of forcing open the larder door, and on another occasion she and the Laird returned to be told, by Hal, that a group of marauding donkeys, possibly led by the one spotted earlier, had made their way into the van, where they ate all the oranges and pears and the newest copy of *Punch*. In the mornings, during the golden half hour after morning tea, Mrs Ratcliffe often saw leopard cubs at play in the ferns and silver jackals running off into the undergrowth. One afternoon, while she sat under the trees, presiding over the teapot in the shade, an emerald snake streaked across her lap and then vanished over her shoulder. Being a woman of quite extraordinary good humour, she found the incident charming.

African tortoises also entranced her. They kept dashing into the road in front of the 'African Marigold' and had to be rescued and placed back in the roadside grass again. They were very active little creatures, which could scuttle along at high speed. There were twelve different varieties, all of which seemed to have the same reckless disregard for life and limb which led them to zoom out at the sound of an approaching caravan and throw themselves under its wheels. Although Mrs Ratcliffe found their behaviour strange, she did not consider them stupid, and she related a native African folk tale to back up her theory that they were actually extremely crafty. One day a tortoise proposed a race between himself and a small kind of antelope, called a durka. When the durka accepted his challenge, the tortoise summoned all his relatives and told them to station themselves along the course that he had

The new caravans had no room for servants: users had to be prepared to set up camp for themselves.

agreed with the antelope, so that as his opponent travelled along he would constantly see a tortoise ahead of him and think that he was losing the race. The plan worked: the antelope ran faster and faster in a desperate attempt to catch up with his rival until he finally dropped dead from exhaustion. Meanwhile the wily tortoise was still sitting at the starting point of the race, basking in the sun.

The 'African Marigold' was subjected to great extremes of weather. For the first part of the trip the sun beat down unmercifully. The party rose early, travelled in the coolest part of the morning, and then camped in the shade of trees in the afternoon, where they spread out their rug and sat with their pot of tea waiting for children to appear out of the surrounding villages and offer to run their errands. Native vendors sold them peaches and plums, melons and grapes from carts pulled along the roads by teams of six or eight donkeys. They always tried to camp near to water, where they could bathe by moonlight if there were enough of a stream to get wet in. Somebody along the way told Mrs Ratcliffe that a South African river was 'a dry place under a railway bridge'. This was a correct description only during the summer months. At the end of December, the 'African Marigold' was pitched on the edge of the bed of the Malpas river, which was a mere trickle passing feebly over baked mud and stones. During the night, the Laird was woken by the sound of a deluge that hit the roof of the van with an almighty sound. He woke the others, then managed to secure the 'African Marigold' to a tree while Mrs Ratcliffe went for help. She returned with enough people to drag the van away from the river to safety, moments before the tree to which it had been tied was swept downstream by the raging river. For the next week it rained solidly, like a curtain, and when it was finally possible to carry on with the tour, the van kept sticking at every ford. At one river-crossing it was hauled out by a team of sixteen mules. On a second occasion it took sixteen oxen to free it from the mire.

None of these disasters troubled Mrs Ratcliffe for a moment; in fact, she grew increasingly cheerful as the tour progressed. Some of her happiest memories centred on the Transkei, which she considered the most beautiful region of South Africa. It was there that she and the Laird had their only real contact with native Africans. They were given an introduction to the Paramount Chief of Pondoland, a man called Victor Poto, whose house was to be found on the way to Durban. Mrs Ratcliffe was keen to meet the chief, and both she and her husband were very disappointed when they finally discovered that his home was nothing more than a small cottage. The chief was out, however, attending a wedding, and the couple decided to persevere in their search to see a Paramount Chief and a tribal ceremony at the same time. After some difficulty, they tracked down the wedding party in the clearing of a village. Half-naked natives danced and drank while old women sat smoking their pipes. The Pondo men often had several wives, for which they paid anything from five to ten oxen, and for each of whom they had to provide a separate hut. The wives seemed to find the arrangement as satisfactory as their husbands, which surprised Mrs Ratcliffe. Several of the young men at the wedding feast asked her if she belonged to the Laird, and invited her to dance with them; she began to feel quite frightened until the chief's interpreter came to her rescue and went to find his master. Chief Victor Poto finally emerged from one of the kraals in the village compound. He was so tall that he had to crawl out through the doorway. He was in European dress and looked like a 'cross between a heavyweight boxer and a prosperous bar-tender'. He was accompanied by his wife, who wore a blue turban and was immensely fat. The Chief explained that he was a Wesleyan and therefore monogamous, but he was clearly very proud of the one wife he had. Mrs Ratcliffe felt that she should offer some form of gift, so she took off the mother-of-pearl necklace that she wore and fastened it around the neck of the chief's wife. For one awful moment she thought that it would be too tight to fasten, but she squeezed it into the rolls of fat and managed to close the clasp. The chief's wife was obviously a popular figure. All the other women of the village jostled their breasts together and laughed as a sign of approval as they watched her receive the gift.

The Laird, who had been very disparaging about natives throughout the trip, and had been heard to grunt ominously when it was suggested that black men were equal in intelligence to whites, became quite jolly with the Pondos. He announced that he had paid one hundred oxen for his wife, and several times he declared it a sensible arrangement that Pondo women should be beaten by their husbands as a sign of affection. He even went so far as to allow his wife to take a photo of him standing in his safari shorts beside three native children, while they all held their hands in the air and gave the Pondo greeting.

While books such as *South African Summer* and articles in magazines brought news back to Britain of intrepid fellow countrymen abroad, an increasing amount of interest was being shown in what the Americans were doing and how the caravan industry was developing in the United States. The initial coverage of progress was slightly patronizing. The shape of American trailer caravans was much rounder than the English version, with V-shaped fronts constructed so that the trailer could be hitched very close to the back of the car for towing purposes. British experts were not keen on the rather bullet-like outlines of these vans, and were somewhat sceptical of the American school of thought that considered it preferable to construct the whole caravan entirely out of light metal. The van industry was still developing its ideas and trying out a series of different methods to suit American requirements. Caravans had not been around for long. The first motor caravans, or 'home cars' as they

'Bayete!' (Hail!) The Laird (Mrs Ratcliffe's spouse) and three South African acquaintances giving the Pondo greeting, after attending a tribal wedding party.

were called in the States, were built in about 1920. They were able to accommodate four people who could sit side by side whilst driving, facing the road, and then disperse at night between one double and two single bunks. Like all American caravans, then and later, they included a refrigerator among the essential features on the floor-plan. The home cars were much larger in 1920 than any of the other traffic on the highways. These were days prior to the advent of large lorries and coaches, and the other tourists on the road found the big motor caravans very objectionable. Later, large trailer coaches were introduced for the commercial transportation of passengers. These were modelled on the home-made trailers that began to appear in the late 1920s, which were themselves heavily influenced by the vans that were made in Britain.

There were a variety of floor-plans, but all of them, no matter how small, included running water, refrigerator and electric light run from the automobile battery. Most did not include a compartment for a lavatory. No one was keen on Elsans, or any other type of portable toilet that had to be emptied, and latrine tents were never even contemplated. American travellers would rather walk half a mile to the nearest gas station to use their facilities than to have a system of their own that required digging duty.

In 1934 the trailer and caravan industry was so small that it barely warranted mention in the British caravan magazine. Within a year, there was an extraordinary surge of interest and the numbers of caravans increased dramatically. In February 1936, 1,094 different trailer outfits attended a convention of the Tin Can Tourists of the World at a trailer park in Sarasota in Florida. The Tin Can Tourists of the World was an organization that had been founded fifteen years earlier by a few charter members. Its rules were simple. Anyone could join if he or she agreed to be a friend in need to fellow motorists on the highway. There were no dues, but there were three annual events for the members to attend: a winter convention, a summer reunion and an annual homecoming. The winter convention was the most exciting of the events, and it was during this meeting that the club officers for the next year were elected. The winter convention was usually held in Sarasota. Florida was the centre of trailer and caravan activity in the States, and the park in Sarasota, where they all congregated, was exceptionally well equipped to meet all their needs. In 1936 the option of permanent membership was introduced. Its price was 50 cents, and this also bought a special card and a lapel button. There was a very definite resistance among Tin Can members to making money out of their organization. No vendors were allowed in the trailer park during the ten days of the convention and no liquor was permitted to be on sale. The atmosphere was friendly, with an emphasis on self-made entertainment. People played shuffleboard, quoits or baseball in the camp grounds. At night local talent and Tin Can members put on free shows for

The ox team at Jägersbosch (South Africa) pulling the car and 'Marigold' across the river, as the bridge and banks had been torn down by floods. The caravan seemed to spend most of its time bogged down in mud or water.

their friends. The whole visit to the convention could cost as little for a member as the $1.25 that was required to rent a site in the park, and this fee granted access to all the amenities on offer in the Sarasota Trailer Park.

These amenities would have been extensive. Sarasota was considered the finest facility in the country, and most large cities, where caravans had scarcely been heard of a year before, had constructed trailer parks by 1936. Part of the reason for the sudden boom was the Depression, which had caused a great many people to move around in search of new lives when their old ones crumbled around them. An article published in a Boston paper in 1935 dubbed the large numbers of travellers who were taking to their vans 'Pneumatic Nomads', and claimed that by staying on the move they were managing to dodge the payment of taxes. The writer quoted the story of a caravanner he had met, the ex vice-president of a trunk- and baggage-making concern who had lost his company and found himself with only a small income and no prospect of future employment. He bought a trailer and had been on the move for the last four years, during which time he had visited 45 states. He reckoned that it cost him $150 a month to live in reasonable comfort, accompanied by his books and his golf clubs. His wife also liked the life and found the trailer camps, which contained grocery stores and laundries, and where there was even a mail delivery, to be very convenient.

At the end of 1936, when the Tin Can Tourists Club could claim 40,000 members, the American journalist Roger Babson predicted that within twenty years half of the population of the United States would be living in automobile trailers. 'The covered-wagon era is living again,' he declared. It was certainly fashionable to be seen in a caravan that year. W.C. Fields had his own two-wheeler trailer that had cost $3000. Buster Keaton's cost him $8000. Gary Cooper painted his blue and had drapes to match, while Joan Blondell, whose trailer had an observation platform at the back, decorated hers in grey with chintz-covered upholstery. English actors and actresses were also taking to trailers, though not with quite the same enthusiasm as their American counterparts. Gracie Fields obligingly smiled from the doorway of her Eccles van for the camera, but she did not seem to find the same magic in the setting as Dick Powell did when he was snapped coming down the steps of his trailer during the filming of *Gold Diggers of 1935*.

In Britain the trailer caravan had become connected in people's minds with budget holidays and weekend jaunts for city girls and their boyfriends. A few elaborate motor caravans could still evoke an aura of glamour and success. There was a brief fashion for double-decker motor vans. The grandest of these offered three upstairs bedrooms, a bathroom and two lavatories, with separate accommodation for the driver and cook in the cab. There were few buyers. The days of the rich eccentrics who wanted to live like gypsies had passed. One or two characters remained, and carried on in the spirit of the pioneers. Most notable of these was Captain J.F. Macmullen, who had a double-decker shooting box designed for him. He named it 'Protos' and drove his wife and friends around in it himself, declaring that it handled better than most of the other cars on the road.

Other caravanners were content to read nostalgic articles about the early days in the caravan magazines. There was a brief flurry of articles about horse-drawn *vardos* and gypsy gentlemen at the time when the Caravan Club, which had struggled through the lean years with a complement of eighty members, most of whom had taken out life membership decades earlier, was relaunched under the auspices of the *Caravan and Trailer* magazine. By the end of the 1930s, the club had 1,400 members: small numbers by American standards of the day, but a huge increase as far as the British caravanning community was concerned. With the founding of the Caravan Council by W.M. Whiteman, a committee designed to help control the steady development of orderly growth in the caravan world, the scene was set for the vast flood of vans that were going to burst out across Britain at the end of the Second World War.

CHAPTER 14

MODERN TIMES

In August 1942 Montgomery, who was still a Lieutenant General at that time, took over from General N.M. Ritchie as commander of the Eighth Army in North Africa. When he arrived he inherited a motor caravan from his predecessor which became his home for almost a year. This van was not British. It had been captured a year earlier from General Annibale 'Electric Whiskers' Bergonzoli when he and his men of the Italian 23rd Corps were defeated at Beda Fromm. It was sent to have its Lancia chassis replaced by one made by Leyland, and then adopted for use in the desert campaign. When Montgomery assumed command in North Africa, he moved into the van and hung pictures on its walls of his four greatest opponents in the war. He had photographs of Kesselring, Model and von Rundstedt, and a pastel portrait of his most deadly foe, Rommel, all looking down at him as he sat and planned his strategy. He said of the pictures: 'I used to look at the photograph of the general I was up against and try to decide what sort of person he was, and how he was likely to react to any moves I might make against him. In some curious way this helped me in the battle.'

The van was sparsely furnished, with only the basic washstand, closets, desk and a couch that doubled up as a bed. Its simplicity appealed to Montgomery. He believed that soft conditions made soldiers fight badly. He insisted that his troops should live and sleep out of doors, in the fields or in the desert, where they were unlikely to become comfortable and complacent. He spent most of his time amongst them, and found the tough life of the army suited his temperament perfectly. He was an ascetic man by nature, who preferred sandwiches to the sort of elaborate supper parties that generals in earlier wars enjoyed, and part of his popularity with his men and his success in battle was due to the spartan and professional atmosphere that he fostered in the areas under his command.

In May of 1943 a second Italian caravan was captured. It was taken from Field Marshal Giovanni Messe, Commander of the First Italian Army, during the final stages of the North African Campaign. Montgomery, who was by now a full General, after the successful battle of El Alamein, was told that Rommel had actually used the van at times. Perhaps the thought that his greatest opponent had slept in the same bed and washed in the same basin now constituting his own private territory gave Montgomery a sense of power and satisfaction. He certainly became very possessive about the new van. After its Lancia chassis had been changed to an American Mack chassis in Tripoli, it became the General's sleeping quarters, while the old van was converted into his office.

'I would turn out of this caravan only for two people. The King [George VI] and Winston Churchill,' he said later.

Both of these men came to see him in the desert during the war. Churchill arrived too early to stay in the van that Rommel had used, but he twice spent the night in 'Electric Whiskers' Bergonzoli's former quarters. On the second visit he was accompanied by his doctor, who was very annoyed at being stuck in a caravan when there were undoubtedly good hotels available in Tripoli. Winston Churchill seemed to be happy enough with the accommodation. Photographs taken at the time showed him sitting, with an amiable expression on his face, chatting in the shade beside the caravan, and admiring the General's new puppy, Rommel. The King came for a four-day visit on 19 June 1943, at which time he presented Montgomery with a knighthood. 'The King is to stay with me at my HQ and my cook is very excited,' Montgomery wrote to a friend at the time.[11] Despite the omission of any reference to his own emotions, and the eminence of the various other visitors that came to the caravan (but not to stay in it) over the years, it is likely that the days with the King were very exciting, not only for the cook, but for the General himself.

By the end of the war caravans were popular with all generals, not just the Italians. Generals Wilson, Paget, Alexander and Dempsey were all photographed at one time or another in theirs. Churchill took time to visit a captured German van called the Viper. The King of Greece was presented with one. Neither it, nor any of the others, were things of beauty in themselves. They were poky and functional in the extreme; their glamour lay in the fact that they were the nerve centres of battle. To catch a general in his van was like finding a fox in his lair.

In January 1944 Montgomery decided that he needed a map lorry from which he could conduct operations in the field. For the first time he ordered a van instead of taking one belonging to an enemy. The caravan he wanted was made up for him by the British Trailer Company to his design, and he then used it as his headquarters in North West Europe. The van was specially equipped with a telephone so that he could speak directly to his subordinate commanders, and had brilliant lighting and black-out curtains to make it usable all through the night. It was one of very few caravans that were specially ordered during the Second World War. Most branches of the Armed Forces used vans extensively, but these were usually either bought or hired

Monty's only purpose-built caravan. Several generals before and after the Second World War used caravans as their living quarters in the field. Camouflage helped to protect the vans from aerial attacks.

Churchill leaving Monty's caravan during the North African campaign, February 1943. Montgomery was only prepared to give up his personal quarters for the Prime Minister or the King.

from dealers and adapted to various purposes. When a specific order was placed, Car Cruisers was the company most likely to receive the business. In 1940, it made a utility van called a Vacuation Van, which was fitted with an anthracite stove. At about the same time another company, Raven, brought out a trailer for emergency accommodation called a Mobile Billet, and a caravan for longer-term use called 'Cheltenham', which had black-out curtains fitted to the windows.

Although some vans were used by military personnel at isolated posts or overcrowded headquarters, many more were the homes of people displaced by war. The biggest problem for the families moving into every shape and size of caravan was caused by condensation. The first three winters of the war were bitterly cold and most of the new vans were either fitted with solid-fuel stoves or had them put in by amateurs who wanted to keep warm. Because most vans had been used for summer vacations, the insulation in the walls was minimal, and the inclusion of a stove was not standard in most models built in the 1930s. When the fire got going the heat rose, and if the van was poorly ventilated or the owners had closed all the vents in a desperate attempt

After the Second World War, holiday-makers began to enjoy travelling in renovated gypsy caravans. It is still possible to rent a vardo *today and take a trip as a gentleman gypsy.*

to save the warmth, then the level of fumes became alarming. The floor might be so cold that it was unbearable to stand on while the air by the ceiling was too stuffy to breathe. Wringing wet mattresses and mouldy clothes added to the miseries of the people who camped out in their vans. Their only consolation was that caravans were remarkably good at withstanding the force of an air raid. Because they were free-standing, they bounced and twisted in the shock waves sent out by bombs, and then landed unscathed on the ground when the attack was over.[12]

The lessons learned by caravan-builders during the war years were put to good use in the new models that appeared in the years that followed. Better ventilated to accommodate the use of stoves, and well insulated to withstand the cold, they were useful to the buyer for longer periods of the year. They were snapped up by a voracious public. Many different groups wanted temporary accommodation for various reasons, and the caravan was often the best solution for their needs. War-time evacuees still stayed on sites in their thousands, to be joined by others who had no home to go back to because of bombing. Workers who were involved in new projects around Great Britain, building houses and factories to replace the ones lost in the war, or moving into one of the many expanding industrial areas developing around the major cities, needed short-term housing in towns that were already full to overflowing. Holiday-makers, including a very considerable group who had been denied paid holidays in the 1930s but were now entitled to them, wanted to go to the seaside.

During the war, the pleasure camps had been used for the internment of prisoners; this, added to the regimented aura that they had about them in the late 1940s, made them unpopular with people who had just spent six years caught up in the rules and regulations of war. Butlins was worried enough to respond to jibes in the press about over-organization with pamphlets which proclaimed that all tastes were catered for. They wrote, 'Now . . . please – please don't – get the idea that you've GOT TO BE GAY at Prestatyn. No compulsion. No chivvying you to do this or that. You are the guest – and it's *your* holiday.'[13]

Even without the *double-entendre* we should find in this advertisement today, the post-war readers responded warily to the publicity handouts. By now they were sophisticated, emancipated, class-conscious and independent. They decided to give the camps a miss and to opt for the freedom offered on caravan sites instead. They did not care if conditions were a bit rough. They had lived through worse; and the fact that there was no landlady breathing down their necks compensated more than adequately for a few difficulties with the plumbing. They were only there for a week or two in any case. They came to the coasts in vast numbers to hire vans on residential sites. In 1955, two million families took caravan holidays. With demand outstripping supply,

Modern gypsies still strictly observe the custom of using two washing-up bowls: one for eating utensils and the other for dirty clothes and dirty bodies.

they played into the hands of wide boys and caravan barons who ran poorly equipped sites at great profit, evicted families at will and operated monopolies so that they could extort premium payments out of people who wanted to stay in their parks. For the poor families who had been left homeless by the war and never got back on their feet or found proper work, it was a miserable life. They could be kicked off their plot in the summer, when better-paying customers could be found, and no one really cared about their plight. Local governments regarded the caravan sites and the people who lived on them as highly undesirable; they were interested only in moving them along as fast as possible. Parks were allowed to continue for a year or so in the Green Belt areas, where they were officially banned by councillors prepared to turn a blind eye to the shanties and tumbledown vans, because they had no alternative accommodation to offer the desperate families that filled them; but before they could become really established, council officials would come in and clear out the sites. The caravan barons were happy with the situation. They made their profits, then set up again in a new location, or waited a while and reopened the condemned sites again. The families that were moved out, however, were left more bereft and separated from society than they had been already. Even in places where the local authorities were prepared to grant permission for parks, this was only given for three-, five- or seven-year periods. This was too short a time to warrant proper capital investment and encouraged the building of inadequate facilities.

The snobbism of some caravanners added to the problem. 'Sporting' tourists looked down on the residential sites and on the families who lived on them. They had no sympathy with people who, as they saw it, spoiled their chances of getting a good pitch when they went touring on their holidays. The two types of caravan-users that were developing were from different social classes and they were bound to feel hostile to each other when their interests clashed. The 'tourers' were particularly cross when they were lumped together with the less fortunate caravanners in a blanket condemnation by the public. Their feelings of superiority were unforgivable, but there were some fundamental differences between the two groups which meant that the only common ground that they shared was the fact that they spent time in caravans. Most vans on residential sites were inhabited by people who wanted either to live or to take a holiday in a house, but could not afford to do so. The tourers used caravans because they wanted to move about, and took their pleasure from the act of travelling. They derived a sense of freedom from living on the road for a while, far from civilization, and they needed to be as isolated as possible to get enjoyment from their tour.

Holiday-makers found their freedom in the unstructured life of the residential sites. On a small budget, they could avoid the hide-bound boarding-houses and stay in a place of their own where they made their own rules. They were often getting away from rented rooms at home, with landlords who watched over their actions, ready to give them notice to quit at the first hint of trouble. In some ways, even if they could have afforded to stay in the smart hotels by the coast, they would have preferred to be in the vans, where they could dress as they pleased, get up late and eat what they liked in a relaxed atmosphere, instead of sitting stiff and silent in a hotel dining-room eating indifferent food under the critical eye of waiters. As for the permanent residents on the sites, freedom of any kind was a luxury that most of them could not afford.

The situation changed gradually. The homeless families were eventually assimilated, to a large extent, into council housing, where they could finally become part of a neighbourhood and put down roots. Caravan sites changed in the 1970s and 1980s. Once they were recognized as a necessary part of the new leisure industry that no one had contemplated in 1940, but which had grown to be one of the major sources of employment within thirty years, the councils brought in legislation for the development of permanent caravan parks, which were tidied up and provided with suitable sanitation and water facilities. With a new awareness of the environment, planners dictated clear instructions to the site-owners. Vans were painted to blend in with the surrounding countryside, and placed, as often as possible, out of view of the roads, so that travelling tourists would have an uninterrupted view of the scenery. Screens of trees were planted. Orderly residents returned year after year to the same spot, where their vans awaited them, ready to be plugged into a general water and electricity supply. The sites were no longer considered a blight, but a welcome addition to the local economy of rural and seaside districts. Whether they also retained any of the romance of the road is debatable.

At the present time, as the country grows crowded and more leisured, it becomes almost impossible to get away from other people. Even the tops of the mountains are packed on bank holidays. There is slightly more chance in the United States, where large numbers of Americans drive to remote areas in luxuriously fitted motor homes, somewhat reminiscent of the old showmen's vans. It is more common there to find men and women who spend their lives on the road, cruising from one trailer park to another as the whim takes them. They certainly do not constitute half the population, as predicted by Roger Babson in the *Los Angeles Times* in 1936, but the covered-wagon era that he wrote about has perhaps been living in the American consciousness ever since the first settlers set off from New England on the way to the Pacific Ocean. Restlessness, adventure, a great desire to see over the next hill and find out if life is better there – all these emotions still keep them on the move.

In Britain, where there is far less uncluttered countryside in which to wander, it is undoubtedly harder to lead a travelling life. Even the gypsies now have to spend most of their time in camps provided by the councils. There is almost no wasteland left. Because of this lack of space we should be grateful that the caravan industry developed as it did after the Second World War, so that the structure was viable in time to deal with the tourist boom. Nowadays many millions of people take their holidays in caravans. They enjoy themselves by the sea or in the woods and mountains without causing great inconvenience to the local population around the areas that they visit. The caravan sites on which they stay are far from beautiful, but they have an enormous advantage over the alternative methods of coping with the huge influx of visitors that are used in other countries. They have no permanent effect on the landscape at all. The coastal areas around the Mediterranean are almost obliterated by the huge conglomerations of hotels that have been thrown up, in haste, along the beaches. Even if all the tourists went home tomorrow and stayed there, it would be impossible to restore those shores to their original state. That is not the case in Great Britain. Caravan parks are, almost by definition, movable and temporary. Take them away, and the sea

Until local councils passed legislation for new and better caravan sites, gypsies and homeless gorgios lived in squalid conditions, subject to the greedy whims of 'caravan barons'.

The conflict between the desire of caravanners for scenic places to camp in and the danger that the presence of caravans will then spoil that scenery has by now largely been solved by the introduction of well-run sites hidden from view.

shores can be seen looking very much the same as they did when Dr Gordon Stables drove the 'Wanderer' to the coast of East Anglia a hundred years ago. It is a wonderful stroke of luck that the countryside has survived the worst ravages of tourism, and although various organizations have been formed during this century to safeguard the environment, it is only fair to recognize that the use of caravans saved many areas of beauty from massive bouts of cheap building construction, and left them in their natural state at times when very few voices were raised in favour of conservation.

The early pioneers of pleasure caravans would be delighted if they knew that they had helped to preserve the wild places of Britain, even if they were bewildered by the number of tourists who nowadays pass through the haunts that they considered to be virtually inaccessible. They might find that the residential sites had little in common with the kind of caravanning that they enjoyed, but they would have found plenty of kindred spirits in the hippies of the 1960s and 1970s. The Simple Lifers would have considered the goals of the wanderers in their Volkswagen vans and psychedelic buses very compatible. Overland travellers like Herbert Shultz could have commiserated with later Englishmen who attempted the journey. The retired civil servant Sir Basil Engholm, who, with his wife Nancy, drove through the desert during the last months of 1977 on the way to India and found himself bogged down in the mud caused by winter rains, in true caravan tradition, might have wished he had read Mr Shultz's warning letter in the *Caravan and Trailer* in 1936 about

Even seen in a muddy squatters' camp, the gypsy caravan looks fine and graceful and will have a spotlessly clean interior.

the dire consequences of attempting the journey in the winter. Like Mr Shultz, the Engholms found the conditions very difficult, and they were amazed that they achieved their objective, even though it took them nine and a half months to reach India and return to England. Unlike the Shultz family, they enjoyed themselves enormously along the way. They often needed assistance on the road, but they were always helped by local people, who treated them with unfailing courtesy. Iranian lorry-drivers rescued them when they were marooned in the desert; Indian forestry workers mended their hard-used springs and would take nothing in payment except a glass of water; a friendly embassy official drove through the night to find them and give warning because he had just heard that the border of Afghanistan was closing after an internal coup; Iraquis held up English textbooks to the caravan windows in a gesture of friendship.

The kind treatment that they received on their journey was not unusual. The same welcome can be found now, by travellers in odd corners of the world. The camaraderie of the road still prevails for people daft enough and courageous enough to set off into the distance with a spare tin of petrol and large-scale map. Every time that one of them decides, for the joy of it, to live on the move for a week, or a month, or forever, something is added to the adventure story that started with the first gentlemen gypsies in their horse-drawn vans. Whatever the differences that time and circumstances have imposed, all these travellers are drawn together by a love of the open road that has as much to do with free-wheeling in the soul as with transport for the body.

FOOTNOTES

1 Duncan, H.O., *The World on Wheels* (published by the author, Paris, 1926).

2 Whitehead, Robert A., *The Age of the Traction Engine* (Ian Allen, 1970).

3 (Also much of the information in Chapter 3): Okely, Judith, *The Traveller-Gypsies*, Changing Culture series (Cambridge University Press, 1983).

4 Holroyd, Michael, *Augustus John: a biography* (Penguin Books; first published by William Heinemann, 1974, 1975 in 2 volumes).

5 Smith, Bertram, *The Whole Art of Caravanning* (Shire Publications, Aylesbury, 1981).

6 Jennings, Frances, *A Tour in a Donkey Cart* (John Lane, The Bodley Head, 1921).

7 *Mr Punch's History of the Great War* (Cassell & Co., 1919).

8 *Mr Punch's History of the Great War* (Cassell & Co., 1919).

9 (Also much of the information on Miss Hasell's life): Fast, Vera, *A Missionary on Wheels: Eva Hasell and the Sunday School Caravan Missions* (The Anglican Book Centre, Toronto, 1979).

10 Knight, Dame Laura, *A Proper Circus Omie* (Peter Davies, 1962).

11 Hamilton, Nigel, *Monty, Master of the Battlefield, 1942–44* (Hamish Hamilton, 1983).

12 Whiteman, W.M., *History of the Caravan* (Blandford Press, 1973).

13 Pimlott, J.A.R., *The Englishman's Holiday: a social history* (Harvester Press, 1947).

BIBLIOGRAPHY

Arnim, Mary Annette von, *The Caravaners* (Smith, Elder & Co., 1909).

Baker, Richard St Barbe, *The Brotherhood of the Trees* (Figurehead, 1930).

Baker, Richard St Barbe, *I Planted Trees* (Lutterworth Press, 1944).

Baker, Sir Samuel White, *Cyprus As I Saw It in 1879* (Macmillan & Co., 1879).

Bankes, George, *Across France in a Caravan* (Blackwood & Sons, 1892).

Benson, E.F., *Winter Sports in Switzerland* (George Allen & Co., 1913).

Bonnett, Harold, *Farming with Steam* (Shire Publications, Aylesbury, 1974).

Bostock, E.H., J.P.F.Z.S., *Menageries, Circuses and Theatres* (Chapman & Hall, 1927).

Boswell, Silvester Gordon, *The Book of Boswell, Autobiography of a Gypsy*, ed. John Seymour (Victor Gollancz, 1970).

Braithewaite, Rev. Robert (ed.), *The Life and Letters of Rev. William Pennefather, B.A.* (John F. Shaw & Co., 1878).

Briggs, Asa, *A Social History of England* (Penguin Books, 1983).

Cameron, L.C.R. *The Book of the Caravan* (L. Upcott Gill, 1907).

Crosby, Ernest, *Edward Carpenter: Poet and Prophet* (*The Conservator*, Philadelphia, 1901).

Cunliffe, Marcus, *History of the Western World*, Vol. 5: *The Age of Expansion, 1848–1917* (Weidenfeld & Nicolson, 1974).

Duncan, H.O., *The World on Wheels* (published by the author, Paris, 1926)

Fast, Vera, *A Missionary on Wheels: Eva Hasell and the Sunday School Caravan Missions* (The Anglican Book Centre, Toronto, 1979).

Gernsheim, Helmut and Alison, *Roger Fenton, Photographer of the Crimean War: his photographs and letters from the Crimea with an essay on his life and work* (Secker & Warburg, 1954).

Grahame, Kenneth, *Wind in the Willows* (Methuen & Co., 1908).

Hamilton, Nigel, *Monty, Master of the Battlefield, 1942–44* (Hamish Hamilton, 1983).

Hasell, F.H. Eva, in collaboration with F.S., *Across the Prairie in a Motor Caravan: a 3,000-mile tour by two Englishwomen on behalf of religious education* (SPCK, 1922).

Hasell, F.H. Eva, *Through Western Canada in a Caravan* (SPG, 1925).

Holroyd, Michael, *Augustus John: a biography* (Penguin Books; first published by William Heinemann, 1974, 1975 in 2 volumes).

Imperial War Museum, Exhibit Leaflet No. 1, *The Montgomery Caravans*.

Jaeger, Gustav, M.D., *Selections from Essays on Health – Culture and the Sanitary Woollen System* (Dr Jaeger's Sanitary Woollen System Co., 1884).

Jennings, Frances, *A Tour in a Donkey Cart* (John Lane, The Bodley Head, 1921).

Knight, Laura, *Oil Paint and Grease Paint: autobiography of Laura Knight* (Ivor Nicholson & Watson, 1936).

Knight, Dame Laura, *A Proper Circus Omie* (Peter Davies, 1962).

Lomax, Alfred E., *Sir Samuel Baker: his life and adventures* (The Sunday School Union, from the Splendid Lives series, 1894).

Lucas, E.V., *The Slowcoach: a story of roadside adventure* (Wells Gardner Darton & Co., 1910).

Munnings, Sir Alfred, K.C.V.O., *An Artist's Life: the autobiography of Sir Alfred Munnings* (Museum Press, 1950–2).

Okely, Judith, *The Traveller-Gypsies*, Changing Culture series (Cambridge University Press, 1983).

Pimlott, J.A.R., *The Englishman's Holiday: a social history* (Harvester Press, 1947).

Priestley, J.B., *The Edwardians* (Heinemann, 1970).

Punch, Mr, *Mr Punch's History of the Great War* (Cassell & Co., 1919).

Ratcliffe, Dorothy Una, *South African Summer: 5000 miles with a Car and Caravan* (Country Life, 1933).

Richardson, Charles, *The New Book of the Horse* (Cassell & Co., 1910).

Rolt, L.T.C., *Isambard Kingdom Brunel: a biography* (Longmans, Green & Co., 1957).

Ryder, M.L., *Sheep and Man* (Duckworth, 1983).

Sellman, Arthur, *Travelling Shows and Roundabouts* (The Oakwood Press, Blandford, 1975).

Semple, Dugald, *Joy in Living: an autobiography* (William McClellan, Glasgow, 1957).

Semple, Dugald, *Life in the Open* (G. Bell & Sons, 1919).

Semple, Dugald, *Living in Liberty, or The Wheelhouse Philosophy* (Alexander Gardner Paisley, 1911).

Smith, Bertram, *The Whole Art of Caravanning* (Shire Publications, Aylesbury, 1981).

Smith, D.J., *Discovering Horse-drawn Caravans* (Shire Publications, Aylesbury, 1981).

Smith, Eleanor, *Life's a Circus* (Longman, Green & Co., 1939).

Smith, Lady Eleanor, *British Circus Life*, with additional material supplied by John Hinde, ed. W.J. Turner (Harrap & Co., 1948).

Stables, Dr William Gordon, *Cruise of the Land Yacht 'Wanderer' or Thirteen Hundred Miles in My Caravan* (Hodder & Stoughton, 1886).

Stone, J. Harris, M.A.F.L.S.F.C.S., *Caravanning and Camping Out* (Herbert Jenkins, 1913; 2nd edition, 1931).

Swinstead, Rev. J. Howard, M.A., *A Parish on Wheels* (Gardner, Darton and Co., 1897).

Ward-Jackson, C.H. and Harvey, Denis E., *The English Gypsy Caravan: its origins, builders, technology and conservation* (David & Charles, Newton Abbot, 1972).

Wells, H.G., *Bealby, a Holiday* (Methuen & Co., 1915).

Whitehead, Robert A., *The Age of the Traction Engine* (Ian Allen, 1970).

Whiteing, Richard, *The Yellow Van* (Hutchinson & Co., 1903).

Of special value throughout the writing of the book has been:

Whiteman, W.M., *The History of the Caravan* (Blandford Press, 1973).

Magazines and newspapers

The War Cry, The Salvation Army, Archives and Research Centre, 101 Queen Victoria Street, London EC4P 4EP.

Caravan and Trailer, 1933–6, published in London.

PICTURE ACKNOWLEDGEMENTS

Aberdeen Art Gallery and Museum, 101.

BBC Hulton Picture Library, 2, 9, 10, 12, 14, 81, 82, 106-7, 108, 112, 141, 145, 146 (bottom), 157, 158, 159, 161, 162, 163, 164, 166, 170, 173, 177, 179, 188, 190, 193, 194, 195.

The Bridgeman Art Library, 99.

The Bridgeman Art Library/Worthing Museum and Art Gallery, 102.

The British Library, 55, 59, 67 (top), 70, 71, 91, 111, 119, 122, 123, 124, 126, 129, 133, 134-5, 136, 144, 146 (top), 150-1, 154, 169, 174, 181, 183.

The Caravan Club, 46-7, 49, 53.

GLC Historic Buildings Department, 34, 35.

Imperial War Museum, 187.

Laing Art Gallery, Newcastle upon Tyne. By arrangement with Tyne and Wear Museums Service, 104.

Limited Editions Club/The Heritage Club, Avon, Connecticut, USA, 103.

Sir Alfred Munnings Art Museum, Dedham, Essex, 97, 98.

Punch Publications Limited, 117.

The Salvation Army International Archives and Research Centre, 62-3, 67 (bottom), 75.

University of Reading, Institute of Agricultural History and Business Press International, 17, 18, 21, 22-3, 24-5, 27.